My Emily Dickinson

By

Susan Howe

NORTH ATLANTIC BOOKS
BERKELEY, CALIFORNIA

My Emily Dickinson

Copyright © 1985 by Susan Howe

ISBN 0-938190-52-0 (paperback)
ISBN 0-938190-53-9 (cloth)

Published by
North Atlantic Books
P.O. Box 12327
Berkeley, California 94712

Cover and book design by Paula Morrison
Typeset in Bembo by Classic Typography
Cover photo of a daguerreotype taken of Emily Dickinson, about 1848

My Emily Dickinson is sponsored by the Society for the Study of Native Arts and Sciences, a nonprofit educational corporation whose goals are to develop an educational and crosscultural perspective linking various scientific, social, and artistic fields; to nurture a holistic view of arts, sciences, humanities, and healing; and to publish and distribute literature on the relationship of mind, body, and nature.

Library of Congress Cataloging in Publication Data
Howe, Susan.
    My Emily Dickinson.

    Includes index.
      1. Dickinson, Emily, 1830–1886.   2. Poets, American—19th century—Biography.   3. Women authors. I. Title.
PS1541.H69   1985   811'.4   85-21648
ISBN 0-938190-53-9
ISBN 0-938190-52-0 (pbk.)

I have retained Emily Dickinson's eccentricities of spelling and punctuation. All texts for her letters and poems are taken from *The Letters of Emily Dickinson* edited by Thomas H. Johnson. I have used his numbering throughout. I believe, and Ralph Franklin's edition of *The Manuscript Books of Emily Dickinson* now shows, that her carefully marked variant suggestions for wording certain poems are quite deliberate. Again I have used Johnson's method of listing and numbering her suggestions for word changes.

I have used the letter L after quotations from the letters to distinguish the letters from the poems.

I have used the 1855 edition of Browning's "Childe Roland to the Dark Tower Came."

Text for Shakespeare quotations is from the edition edited by Charles Knight. The Dickinson family owned the eight volume Knight edition.

I want to thank Quincy Howe, Barbara Folsom, and Maureen Owen for their help in correcting and proof-reading the manuscript.

It is the women above all—there never have been women, save pioneer Katies; not one in flower save some moonflower Poe may have seen, or an unripe child. Poets? Where? They are the test. But a true woman in flower, never. Emily Dickinson, starving of passion in her father's garden, is the very nearest we have ever been—starving.

Never a woman: never a poet. That's an axiom. Never a poet saw sun here.

(William Carlos Williams,
In The American Grain.)

INTRODUCTION:

My book is a contradiction of its epigraph.

Emily Dickinson once wrote to Thomas Wentworth Higginson; "Candor–my Preceptor–is the only wile." This is the right way to put it.

In his Introduction to *In the American Grain*, William Carlos Williams said he had tried to rename things seen. I regret the false configuration–under the old misappellation–of Emily Dickinson. But I love his book.

The ambiguous paths of kinship pull me in opposite ways at once.

As a poet I feel closer to Williams' writing about writing, even when he goes haywire in "Jacataqua," than I do to most critical studies of Dickinson's work by professional scholars. When Williams writes: "Never a woman, never a poet. . . . Never a poet saw sun here," I think that he says one thing and means another. A poet is never just a woman or a man. Every poet is salted with fire. A poet is a mirror, a transcriber. *Here* "we have salt in ourselves and peace one with the other."

When Thoreau wrote his Introduction to *A Week on the Concord and Merrimack Rivers*, he ended by remembering how he had often stood on the banks of the Musketaquid, or Grass-ground River English settlers had re-named Concord. The Concord's current followed the same law in a system of time and all that is known. He liked to watch this current that was for him an emblem of all progress. Weeds under the surface bent gently downstream shaken by watery wind. Chips, sticks, logs, and even tree stems drifted past. There came a day at the end of the summer or the beginning of autumn, when he resolved to launch a boat from shore and let the river carry him.

Emily Dickinson is my emblematical Concord River.

I am heading toward certain discoveries. . . .

Part One

When I am through the old oak forest gone –
                (John Keats, from "On sitting down to
        read *King Lear* once Again." The sonnet
        was included in a letter to his brothers,
                George and Tom Keats, Friday, 23rd
                                        January 1818.)

Little Cousins,
    Called back.
        Emily.
                (Emily Dickinson's last letter, written to
        her cousins, Louise and Frances Norcross,
                                        May 1886.)

In the college library I use there are two writers whose work refuses to conform to the Anglo-American literary traditions these institutions perpetuate. Emily Dickinson and Gertrude Stein are clearly among the most innovative precursors of modernist poetry and prose, yet to this day canonical criticism from Harold Bloom to Hugh Kenner persists in dropping their names and ignoring their work. Why these two pathfinders were women, why American – are questions too often lost in the penchant for biographical detail that "lovingly" muffles their voices. One, a recluse, worked without encouragement or any real interest from her family and her peers. Her poems were unpublished in her lifetime. The other, an influential patron of the arts, eagerly courted publicity, thrived on company, and lived to enjoy her own literary celebrity. Dickinson and Stein meet each other along paths of the Self that begin and end in contradiction. This surface scission is deceptive. Writing was the world of each woman. In a world of exaltation of *his* imagination, feminine inscription seems single and sudden.

As poetry changes itself it changes the poet's life. Subversion attracted the two of them. By 1860 it was as impossible for Emily Dickinson simply to translate English poetic tradition as it was for Walt Whitman. In prose and in poetry she explored the implications of breaking the law just short of breaking off communication with a reader. Starting from scratch, she exploded habits of standard human intercourse in her letters, as she cut across the customary chronological linearity of poetry. Gertrude Stein (1874–1946), influenced by Cézanne, Picasso and Cubism, verbally elaborated on visual invention. She reached in words for new vision formed from the process of naming, as if a first woman were sounding, not describing, "space of time filled with moving." Repetition, surprise, alliteration, odd rhyme and rhythm, dislocation, deconstruction. To restore the original clarity of each word-skeleton both women lifted the load of European literary custom. Adopting old strategies, they reviewed and re-invented them.

Emily Dickinson and Gertrude Stein also conducted a skillful and ironic investigation of patriarchal authority over literary history. Who polices questions of grammar, parts of speech, connection, and connotation? Whose order is shut inside the structure of a sentence? What inner articulation releases the coils and complications of Saying's assertion? In very different ways the countermovement of these two women's work penetrates to the indefinite limits of written communication.

*   *   *

"The Laugh of the Medusa" by the French feminist Hélène Cixous is an often eloquent plan for what women's writing *will* do. The problem is that *will* too quickly becomes *must*. She writes. "I write woman: woman must write woman. And man, man."

> We don't fawn around the supreme hole. We have no womanly reason to pledge allegiance to the negative. The feminine (as the poets suspected) affirms: " . . . And yes," says Molly, carrying *Ulysses* off beyond any book and toward the new writing; "I said yes, I will Yes."
>   ("Utopias," *New French Feminisms*, p. 255)

But Cixous, the author of *The Exile of James Joyce*, ignores Gertrude Stein, whose *Three Lives* published in 1908, and *The Making of Americans* written between 1907 and 1911, had already carried their author beyond any book before *Ulysses* and after. In the 765 pages of Richard Ellmann's exhaustive biography of Joyce, there are only three brief references to Stein. The first, on page 543, puts her down at once. Mary Column reports that Joyce, when asked his opinion of his famous contemporary and neighbor, answered. "I hate intellectual women." What a world of irony lies under that remark. *Ulysses* was published by Sylvia Beach's Shakespeare and Company; all but four episodes had first appeared in Margaret Anderson's *The Little Review*, and Harriet Weaver financially supported the writer and his family during the years he worked on the book. All three were intellectual women. Molly Bloom may have said "Yes" to the future of new writing, but she was a character not an author. For her author, the intellectual future was masculine. All the elements that Cixous longs for in the writing women *will* do, can be found in Stein, who clearly broke the codes that negated her. Why has she even here been "omitted, brushed aside at the scene of inheritances?"

Sandra M. Gilbert and Susan Gubar are perceptive about the problems and achievements of nineteenth century British novelists who were women. Sadly their book, *The Madwoman in the Attic: The Woman Writer and the Nineteenth Century Literary Imagination*, fails to discuss the implications of a nineteenth century American penchant for linguistic decreation ushered in by their representative poet Emily Dickinson. For these two feminist scholars a writer may conceal or confess all, if she does it in a logical syntax. Emily Dickinson suggests that the language of the heart has quite another grammar. This acutist lyric poet sings the sound of the imagination as learner and founder, sings of liberation into an order beyond gender where "Love is it's own rescue, for we—at our supremest, are but it's trembling Emblems—" (L522)

Givens of Dickinson's life: her sex, class, education, inherited character traits, all influences, all chance events—all carry the condition for her work in their wake. To release those gestures of intention that make her poems great, she chose for some reason to shut herself inside her childhood family constellation. This self-imposed exile, indoors, emancipated her from all representations of calculated human order. Most literary criticism is based on calculations of interest. The reductivist approach to writing signalled by the title of their book forces Sandra M. Gilbert and Susan Gubar to worry unnecessarily that Dickinson chose not to celebrate and sing herself with Whitman; nor could she declare confidently with Emerson that " . . . the Poet is the sayer, the namer, and represents beauty. He is a sovereign, and stands on the centre." She said something subtler. "Nature is a Haunted House—but Art—a House that tries to be haunted." (L459)

Yes, gender difference does affect our use of language, and we constantly confront issues of difference, distance, and absence, when we write. That doesn't mean I can relegate women to what we "should" or "must" be doing. Orders suggest hierarchy and category. Categories and hierarchies suggest property. My voice formed from my life belongs to no one else. What I put into words is no longer my possession. Possibility has opened. The future will forget, erase, or recollect and deconstruct every poem. There is a mystic separation between poetic vision and ordinary living. The conditions for poetry rest outside each life at a miraculous reach indifferent to worldly chronology.

* * *

Where the stitching of suicide simply gathers the poet's scattered selves
into the uniform snow of death, the spider artist's artful stitching connects those fragments with a single self-developed and self-developing
yarn of pearl. The stitch of suicide is a stab or puncture, like a "stitch
in the side." The stitch of art is provident and healing, "a stitch in
time." Stabbing, wounding, the stitch of suicide paradoxically represents
not just a unifying but a further rending. Healing, the stitch of art is
a bridge. . . . But the cleaving of "I felt a Cleaving in my Mind" and
the chasm of "This Chasm, Sweet," are patched and mended, seam
to seam, by the magical stitchery of art.

(*The Madwoman in the Attic*, p. 639)

Who is this Spider-Artist? Not *my* Emily Dickinson. This is poetry
not life, and certainly not sewing. Over a hundred years ago Dickinson
marked this passage in her copy of Elizabeth Barrett Browning's *Aurora
Leigh*:

By the way,
The works of women are symbolical.
We sew, sew, prick our fingers, dull our sight,
Producing what? A pair of slippers, sir,
To put on when you're weary – or a stool
To stumble over and vex you . . . 'curse that stool!'
Or else at best, a cushion, where you lean
And sleep, and dream of something we are not
But would be for your sake. Alas, alas!
This hurts most, this – that, after all, we are paid
The worth of our work, perhaps.

(*Aurora Leigh*, 3, ll. 455–469)

The Spider-Woman spinning with yarn of pearl, whose use of
horizontal dashes instead of ordinary punctuation in her poems is here
described as being "neater and more soigné in manuscript than in
type . . . tiny and clear . . . fine thoughts joining split thoughts theme
to theme," was an artist as obsessed, solitary, and uncompromising
as Cézanne. Like him she was ignored and misunderstood by her own
generation, because of the radical nature of her work. During this
Spider's lifetime there were many widely read "poetesses."

*   *   *

Wallace Stevens said that ''Poetry is a scholar's art.'' It is for some. It was for Dickinson. For nineteenth century women of her class, the word *scholar* signified power. The word suggested closed clubs. Scholar was ''other.'' Scholar was male. In the Victorian New England middle and upper class world of expansive intellectual gesturing, men gesticulated and lectured, while women sat in parlors or lecture halls *listening*. Women like Elizabeth Barrett Browning and George Eliot were the rare exception, and they suffered agonies of insecurity about daring to speak more than ''Lady's Greek, without the accents.''

If *scholar* was an uncertain word, *love* was more uncertain. In the nineteenth century, sensuality too often ushered in tragedy for the female sex. Women from all classes and countries risked dying in childbirth or from infection afterwards. If the mother survived, frequently her baby did not. Between 1861 and 1870 only one British infant in eight survived its first year of life, and as many again died between the ages of one and five. In America the appalling statistics were similar. The spectre of child mortality haunted every family. Uncertain relation of opposition–Love and Death; for men the fusion was metaphysical and metaphorical. Centuries of tropes and clever punning in Western literary tradition have married and mated their meanings. Wedding. Procreation. Who was creator? When creation? The following poems matched with one another, play a scene of domestic libidinal disorder:

HE]MILTON
1658

METHOUGHT I saw my late espoused Saint
   Brought to me like Alcestis from the grave,
   Whom Joves great Son to her glad Husband gave,
   Rescu'd from death by force though pale and faint.
Mine as whom washt from spot of child-bed taint,
   Purification in the old Law did save,
   And such, as yet once more I trust to have
Full sight of her in Heaven without restraint,
Came vested all in white, pure as her mind:
   Her face was vail'd, yet to my fancied sight,
   Love, sweetness, goodness, in her person shin'd
So clear, as in no face with more delight.
   But O as to embrace me she enclin'd
   I wak'd, she fled, and day brought back my night.
         (''Sonnet,'' *on His Deceased Wife)*

SHE]DICKINSON This Chasm, Sweet, upon my life
1864   I mention it to you,
               When Sunrise through a fissure drop
               The Day must follow too.

               If we demur, it's gaping sides
               Disclose as 'twere a Tomb
               Ourself am lying straight within
               The Favorite of Doom.

               When it has just contained a Life
               Then, Darling, it will close
               And yet so bolder every Day
               So turbulent it grows

               I'm tempted half to stitch it up
               With a remaining Breath
               I should not miss in yielding, though
               To Him, it would be Death—

               And so I bear it big about
               My Burial—before
               A Life quite ready to depart
               Can harass me no more—

                                           (858)

    In 1864 was marriage Epithalamion or entrapment? Is Death a soothing mother or a mastiff-father? Is Awe Nature; and destruction the beginning of every Foundation? Do words flee their meaning? Define definition.

1864]   Love—is anterior to Life—
               Posterior—to Death—
               Initial of Creation, and
               The Exponent of Earth—

                                           (917)

    Initial of creation. In the beginning was the Word. Relation of opposition; misprision—double meaning and uncertain.

TITANIA   But she, being mortal, of that boy did die, . . .

QUINCE   Bless thee, Bottom, bless thee! Thou art translated.
                           (*A Midsummer Night's Dream*, II, i, & III, i.)

> That Distance was between Us
> That is not of Mile or Main –
> The Will it is that situates –
> Equator – never can –
>
> (863)

Does a woman's mind move in time with a man's? What is the end of Logic?

Between 1858 and 1860 Emily Dickinson became the poet we know. For this northern will to become *I* – free to excavate and interrogate definition, the first labor called for was to sweep away the pernicious idea of poetry as embroidery for women.

*   *   *

IDENTITY AND MEMORY

> That sacred Closet when you sweep –
> Entitled "Memory" –
> Select a reverential Broom –
> And do it silently.
>
> 'Twill be a Labor of surprise –
> Besides Identity
> Of other Interlocutors
> A probability –
>
> August the Dust of that Domain –
> Unchallenged – let it lie –
> You cannot supersede itself
> But it can silence you –
>
> (1273)

Is this a poem about Memory or is it about the identity of an American woman writing English poetry? So many of Dickinson's poems are about the process of writing, yet even David Porter, one of her most thoughtful critical interpreters, faults her for being without an "*ars poetica.*" Identity and memory are crucial for anyone writing poetry. For women the field is still dauntingly empty. How do I, choosing messages from the code of others in order to participate in the universal theme of Language, pull SHE from all the myriad symbols and sightings of HE. Emily Dickinson constantly asked this question in her poems.

> In lands I never saw–they say
> Immortal Alps look down–
> Whose Bonnets touch the firmament–
> Whose Sandals touch the town–
>
> Meek at whose everlasting feet
> A Myriad Daisy play–
> Which, Sir, are you and which am I
> Upon an August day?
>
>   (124)

Is this a poem about writing a poem or cosmic speculation? Is the space of time constantly changing?

> Staking our entire Possession
> On a Hair's result–
> Then–Seesawing–coolly–on it–
> Trying if it split–
>
>   (971, v. 4)

Spenser made Mutability a woman. Staking and seesawing. To balance on a precipice of falling into foolishness was often the danger of opening your mouth to speak if you were an intellectually ambitious person with a female education. Emily Dickinson chose to stay at home when Ralph Waldo Emerson visited her brother's house next door. One unchosen American woman alone at home and choosing. American authors reverently swept the dust of England's intellectual domain. Meek at whose feet did this myriad American Daisy play? August sun above, below the searing heat of a New England summer. "*Salad days when I was green in judgement* . . . " silent judgment of the august past might challenge you if you challenged it. Might and might . . . wandering through zones of tropes, World filtered through books–*And I and Silence some strange race–Wrecked solitary here–* I, CODE and SHELTER might say one thing to mean the other. An American woman with Promethean ambition might know better than anyone how to let the august traces (domain of dust) lie.

*   *   *

The look of the words as they lay in the print I shall never forget. Not their face in the casket could have had the eternity to me. Now, *my* George Eliot. The gift of belief which her greatness denied her, I trust she receives in the childhood of the kingdom of heaven. As childhood is earth's confiding time, perhaps having no childhood, she lost her way to the early trust, and no later came. Amazing human heart, a syllable can make to quake like jostled tree, what infinite for thee?

(L710)

Dickinson said this in a letter to her Norcross cousins after she had seen the death notice in the paper of one of her favorite authors. Earlier she had said of George Eliot: "She is the lane to the Indes, Columbus was looking for" (L456). What did this female Columbus crossing an uncharted fictive ocean find in George Eliot that made her the lane to the Indies rather than Harriet Beecher Stowe or Margaret Fuller, her own country-women, or even Elizabeth Barrett Browning, her fellow poet?

George Eliot (Mary Ann Evans) was raised in a strict evangelical household. Later in life, she refused to attend church, a rebellion taken very seriously by her family. Although their disapproval cost her great emotional suffering, she remained an agnostic, despite her deep sympathy for the strength of religious motives and her fascination with the history of religion. George Eliot laboriously educated herself, and came late to her calling as a novelist. Eliot maintained her unwavering skepticism, even after reaching the pinnacle of literary celebrity in her lifetime, skepticism so strong that it forced her time and again to pull the rug out from under her most appealing heroines. George Eliot was a brilliant scholar, linguist, and critic; but her fictional scholars wander through a wasteland of languages to encounter only reversals and false definitions. Eliot defied Victorian convention by openly living with a married man. She was furious at the double bind an educated woman, given intellectual aspiration, was placed in by being expected to efface her intellectual drive in the role of servant/mother to the reigning male culture. George Eliot believed that there were different voices for both sexes, and scorned women who congealed into the literary mold men made for them.

By a peculiar thermometric adjustment, when a woman's talent is at zero, journalistic approbation is at the boiling pitch; when she attains mediocrity, it is already at no more than summer heat; and if ever she reaches excellence, critical enthusiasm drops to the freezing point. Harriet Martineau, Currer Bell, and Mrs. Gaskell have been treated as cavalierly as if they had been men. . . . In the majority of women's books you see that kind of facility which springs from the absence of any high standard; that fertility in imbecile combination or feeble imitation which a little self-criticism would check and reduce to barenness. . . .

Happily we are not dependent on argument to prove that fiction is a department of literature in which women can, after their kind, fully equal men. A cluster of great names, both living and dead, rush to our memories in evidence that women can produce novels not only fine, but among the very finest;–novels, too, that have a precious specialty, lying quite apart from masculine aptitudes and experience. No educational restrictions can shut women out from the materials of fiction, and there is no species of art which is so free from rigid requirements. Like crystalline masses, it may take any form, and yet be beautiful; we have only to pour in the right elements–genuine observation, humour, and passion.

("Silly Novels by Lady Novelists," pp. 322–325)

Emerson said the American scholar "must be an inventor to read well. . . . He that would bring home the wealth of the Indies, must carry out the wealth of the Indies." Emily Dickinson across the ocean from George Eliot and Elizabeth Barrett Browning was isolated, inventing, SHE, and American. Isolation in nineteenth century England and America was spelled the same way, but there the resemblance stopped. Poe, Melville, and Dickinson all knew the falseness of comparing. Stevens and Olson later–the boundless westwardness of everything. Ancestral theme of children flung out into memory unknown.

> Four Trees–upon a solitary Acre–
> Without Design
> Or Order, or Apparent Action–
> Maintain–
>
> The Sun–upon a Morning meets them–
> The Wind–
> No nearer Neighbor–have they–
> But God–

The Acre gives them–Place–
They–Him–Attention of Passer by–
Of Shadow, or of Squirrel, haply–
Or Boy–

What Deed is Their's unto the General Nature–
What Plan
They severally–retard–or further–
Unknown–

(742)

3. Action] signal–/notice
4. Maintain] Do reign–
13. is Their's] they bear
15. retard–or further] promote–or hinder–

This is the *process* of viewing Emptiness without design or plan, neighborless in winter blank, or blaze of summer. This is waste wilderness. Nature no soothing mother, Nature is annihilation brooding over.

*   *   *

Emily Dickinson took the scraps from the separate "higher" female education many bright women of her time were increasingly resenting, combined them with voracious and "unladylike" outside reading, and used the combination. She built a new poetic form from her fractured sense of being eternally on intellectual borders, where confident masculine voices buzzed an alluring and inaccessible discourse, backward through history into aboriginal anagogy. Pulling pieces of geometry, geology, alchemy, philosophy, politics, biography, biology, mythology, and philology from alien territory, a "sheltered" woman audaciously invented a new grammar grounded in humility and hesitation. HESITATE from the Latin, meaning to stick. Stammer. To hold back in doubt, have difficulty speaking. "*He* may pause but *he* must not hesitate" –*Ruskin*. Hesitation circled back and surrounded everyone in that confident age of aggressive industrial expansion and brutal Empire building. Hesitation and Separation. The Civil War had split American in two. *He* might pause, *She* hesitated. Sexual, racial, and geographical separation are at the heart of Definition. Tragic and eternal dichotomy–if we concern ourselves with the deepest Reality, is this world of the imagina-

tion the same for men and women? What voice when we hesitate and
are silent is moving to meet us?

> The Spirit is the Conscious Ear.
> We actually Hear
> When We inspect – that's audible –
> That is admitted – Here –
>
> For other Services – as Sound –
> There hangs a smaller Ear
> Outside the Castle – that Contain –
> The other – only – Hear –
>
> (733)
>
> 5. Services] purposes
> 6. smaller] minor
> 7. Castle] Centre – / City
> 7. Contain] present –

At the center of Indifference I feel my own freedom . . . the Liberty
in wavering. Compression of possibility tensing to spring. Might and
might . . . mystic illumination of analogies . . . instinctive human sup-
position that any word may mean its opposite. Occult tendency of oppo-
sites to attract and merge. *Hesitation of us all*, one fire-baptized soul
was singing.

> In many and reportless places
> We feel a Joy –
> Reportless, also, but sincere as Nature
> Or Deity –
>
> It comes, without a consternation –
> Dissolves – the same –
> But leaves a sumptuous Destitution –
> Without a Name –
>
> Profane it by a search – we cannot
> It has no home –
> Nor we who having once inhaled it –
> Thereafter roam.
>
> (1382)
>
> 6. Dissolves] abates – / Exhales –
> 7. sumptuous] blissful
> 9. a search] pursuit
> 11. inhaled it] waylaid it

On this heath wrecked from Genesis, nerve endings quicken. Naked sensibility at the extremest periphery. Narrative expanding contracting dissolving. Nearer to know less before afterward schism in sum. No hierarchy, no notion of polarity. Perception of an object means loosing and losing it. Quests end in failure, no victory and sham questor. One answer undoes another and fiction is real. Trust absence, allegory, mystery–the setting not the rising sun is Beauty. No titles or numbers for the poems. That would force order. No titles for the packets she sewed the poems into. No manufactured print. No outside editor/"robber." Conventional punctuation was abolished not to add "soigné stitchery" but to subtract arbitrary authority. Dashes drew liberty of interruption inside the structure of each poem. Hush of hesitation for breath and for breathing. Empirical domain of revolution and revaluation where words are in danger, dissolving . . . only Mutability certain.

> I saw no Way–The Heavens were stitched–
> I felt the Columns close–
> The Earth reversed her Hemispheres–
> I touched the Universe–
>
> And back it slid–and I alone–
> A Speck upon a Ball–
> Went out upon Circumference–
> Beyond the Dip of Bell–
>
> (378)

*   *   *

Did you ever read one of her Poems backward, because the plunge from the front overturned you? I sometimes (often have, many times) have–A something overtakes the Mind–

(Prose Fragment 30)

We must travel abreast with Nature if we want to know her, but where shall be obtained the Horse–
A something overtakes the mind–we do not hear it coming

(Prose Fragment 119)

Found among her papers after her death, these two fragments offer a hint as to Emily Dickinson's working process. Whether 'her' was

Elizabeth Barrett Browning or Emily Brontë is unimportant. What is interesting is that she found sense in the chance meeting of words. Forward progress disrupted reversed. Sense came after suggestion. *The Years and Hours of Emily Dickinson* by Jay Leyda, and Richard Sewell's meticulously researched *Life of Emily Dickinson*, are invaluable sources of information about her living, but the way to understand her writing is through her reading. This sort of study, standard for most male poets of her stature, is only recently beginning. Ruth Miller and Joanne Feit Diehl have written thoughtful and thoroughly researched books on the subject. Albert Gelpi's *Emily Dickinson and the Deerslayer: The Dilemma of the Woman Poet in America* is too short, but it opens the important question of the influence an American writer like James Fenimore Cooper had on her poems, particularly on the crucial "My Life had stood–a Loaded Gun–." I have tried to take his idea a step further, from *The Deerslayer* to the other Leatherstocking novels. Ralph Franklin's recent facsimile edition has at last made available to readers Dickinson's particular intentions for the order the poems were to be read in. But a proliferaton of silly books and articles continue to disregard this great writer's working process. Is it because a poet-scholar in full possession of *her* voice won't fit the legend of deprivation and emotional disturbance embellished and enlarged on over the years, with the help of books like John Cody's reprehensible biographical psychoanalysis? *After Great Pain* is the rape of a great poet. That Sandra M. Gilbert and Susan Gubar continue to draw on his dubious and reductivist conclusions, and even seem to agree with him in places, is a sorry illustration of the continuing vulgarization of the lives of poets, pandering to the popular sentiment that they are society's fools and madwomen.

                    *   *   *

To recipient unknown   *about 1861*

Master.

    If you saw a bullet hit a Bird–and he told you he was'nt shot– You might weep at his courtesy, but you would certainly doubt his word.
    One drop more from the gash that stains your Daisy's bosom– then would you *believe?* . . .

                            (L233, from second "Master" letter)

> Day and night
> I worked my rhythmic thought, and furrowed up
> Both watch and slumber with long lines of life
> Which did not suit their season. The rose fell
> From either cheek, my eyes globed luminous
> Through orbits of blue shadow, and my pulse
> Would shudder along the purple-veinèd wrist
> Like a shot bird.
> (*Aurora Leigh*, 3, ll. 272–279)

'You'll take a high degree at college, Steerforth,' said I, 'if you have not done so already; and they will have good reason to be proud of you.'

'*I* take a degree!' cried Steerforth. 'Not I! my dear Daisy – will you mind my calling you Daisy?'

'Not at all!' said I.

'That's a good fellow! My dear Daisy,' said Steerforth, laughing, 'I have not the least desire or intention to distinguish myself in that way. I have done quite sufficient for my purpose. I find that I am heavy company enough for myself as I am.'

'But the fame – ' I was beginning.

'You romantic Daisy!' said Steerforth, laughing still more heartily; 'why should I trouble myself, that a parcel of heavy-headed fellows may gape and hold up their hands? Let them do it at some other man. There's fame for him, and he's welcome to it.'

(*David Copperfield*, ch. 20)

Much discussion has centered around the three enigmatic "Master" letters written in the early 1860s and found among Dickinson's posthumous papers. There is no evidence that these letters, written when she was at the height of her creative drive, were ever actually sent to anyone. Discussion invariably centers around the possible identity of the recipient. More attention should be paid to the structure of the letters, including the direct use of ideas, wording, and imagery from both *Aurora Leigh* and *David Copperfield*; imagery most often taken from the two fictional characters, Marian Earle in Barrett Browning's poem and Little Em'ly in Dickens' novel, who are "fallen women." Dickinson's love for the writing of Charles Dickens has been documented, but not well enough. It is a large and fascinating subject, beginning with the chance

similarity of their last names, and the obsession both writers shared
for disguising and allegorical naming. Her letters to Samuel Bowles,
in particular, are studded with quotations and direct references to
characters and passages from Dickens. There is only space to touch on
certain echoes here. In *Aurora Leigh*, Marian Earle describes her passion for Romney:

> She told me she had loved upon her knees,
> As others pray, more perfectly absorbed
> In the act and inspiration. She felt his
> For just his uses, not her own at all, –
> His stool, to sit on or put up his foot,
> His cup, to fill with wine or vinegar,
> Whichever drink might please him at the chance,
> For that should please her always: let him write
> His name upon her . . . it seemed natural;
> It was most precious, standing on his shelf,
> To wait until he chose to lift his hand.
>   (*Aurora Leigh*, 6, ll. 904–905)

In *David Copperfield*, Little Em'ly writes three disjointed, pleading
letters after eloping with Steerforth, addressed to her family, Ham, and
possibly Master Davy/David/Daisy–the recipient is never directly
specified, and the letters are unsigned:

> Oh, if you knew how my heart is torn. If even you, that I have
> wronged so much, that never can forgive me, could only know what
> I suffer! I am too wicked to write about myself. Oh, take comfort in
> thinking that I am so bad. Oh, for mercy's sake, tell uncle that I never
> loved him half so dear as now. Oh, don't remember how affectionate
> and kind you have all been to me–don't remember we were ever to
> be married–but try to think as if I died when I was little, and was buried
> somewhere. . . . God bless all! I'll pray for all, often, on my knees.
>   (DC, ch. 31)

To recipient unknown   *early 1862(?)*

> Oh, did I offend it– . . . Daisy–Daisy–offend it–who bends her
> smaller life to his (it's) meeker (lower) every day–who only asks–a task–
> [who] something to do for love of it–some little way she cannot guess

to make that master glad–. . . .
    Low at the knee that bore her once unto [royal] wordless rest [now]
Daisy [stoops a] kneels a culprit–tell her her [offence] fault–Master–if
it is [not so] small eno' to cancel with her life, [Daisy] she is satisfied–
but punish [do not] dont banish her–shut her in prison, Sir–only pledge
that you will forgive–sometime–before the grave, and Daisy will not
mind–She will awake in [his] your likeness.
                                        (L248, from third "Master" Letter)

    Attention should be paid to Dickinson's brilliant masking and
unveiling, her joy in the drama of pleading. Far from being the hysterical
jargon of a frustrated and rejected woman to some anonymous
"Master"-Lover, these three letters were probably self-conscious exer-
cises in prose by one writer playing with, listening to, and learning
from others.

                        *   *   *

                The Martyr Poets–did not tell–
                But wrought their Pang in syllable–
                That when their mortal name be numb–
                Their mortal fate–encourage Some–
                The Martyr Painters–never spoke–
                Bequeathing–rather–to their Work–
                That when their conscious fingers cease–
                Some seek in Art–the Art of Peace–
                                        (544)
                3. name] fame
                8. Some] Men–

    In some sense the subject of any poem is the author's state of mind
at the time it was written, but facts of an artist's life will never explain
that particular artist's truth. Poems and poets of the first rank remain
mysterious. Emily Dickinson's life was language and a lexicon her landscape. The vital distinction between concealment and revelation is the
essence of her work.

                        *   *   *

> For a Tear is an Intellectual thing;
> And a Sigh is the Sword of an Angel King
> And the bitter groan of a Martyrs woe
> Is an Arrow from the Almighties Bow!
> (Blake, *Jerusalem*, ch. 2 "To the Deists")

HER INTELLECTUAL CONSCIENCE

Must never be underestimated. A tear is an intellectual thing. Dickinson ignored the worst advice from friends who misunderstood the intensity of her drive to simplicity, and heeded the best, culled from her own reading. Her talent was synthetic; she used other writers, grasped straws from the bewildering raveling of Being wherever and whenever she could use them. Crucial was her ability to spin straw into gold. Her natural capacity for assimilation was fertilized by solitude. The omnivorous gatherer was equally able to reject. To find affirmation in renunciation and to be (herself) without. Outside authority, eccentric and unique.

To T. W. Higginson   *November 1871*

I did not read Mr Miller because I could not care about him – Transport is not urged –

Mrs Hunt's Poems are stronger than any written by Women since Mrs – Browning, with the exception of Mrs Lewes – but truth like Ancestor's Brocades can stand alone – You speak of "Men and Women." That is a broad Book – "Bells and Pomegranates" I never saw but have Mrs Browning's endorsement. While Shakespeare remains Literature is firm –

An Insect cannot run away with Achilles' Head. Thank you for having written the "Atlantic Essays." They are a fine joy – though to possess the ingredient for Congratulation renders congratulation superfluous.

Dear friend, I trust you as you ask – If I exceed permission, excuse the bleak simplicity that knew no tutor but the North. Would you but guide

Dickinson

(L368)

*   *   *

Jay Leyda tells us that she marked this passage in her family's eight volume edition of *The Comedies, Histories, Tragedies, and Poems of William Shakespeare*, edited by Charles Knight.

> He that is robb'd, not wanting what is stolen,
> Let him not know't, and he's not robb'd at all.
>   (*Othello*, III,iii)

Forcing, abbreviating, pushing, padding, subtracting, riddling, interrogating, re-writing, she pulled text from text.

*   *   *

Part Two

CHILDE EMILY TO THE DARK TOWER CAME

My Life had stood - a
Loaded Gun -
In Corners - till a day
the Owner passed - identified -
And carried Me away -

And now We roam + in
Sovreign Woods -
And now We hunt the Doe -
And every time I speak
for Him -
the Mountains straight reply -

And do I smile, such
Cordial light
Upon the Valley glow -
It is as a Vesuvian face
Had let its pleasure through -

And when at Night - Our
Good Day done -

I guard My Master's Head.
'Tis better than the Eider-
duck's
+ deep Pillow - to have shared.

To foe of His - I'm deadly
foe -
None + stir the second time
On whom I lay a Yellow
Eye -
Or an emphatic Thumb -

Though I than He - may
longer live
He longer must - than I -
For I have but the + power
to kill,
Without - the power to die -

+ the - + Core + harm + Art-

Ninth Poem in Fascicle 34.

My Life had stood–a Loaded Gun–
In Corners–till a Day
The Owner passed–identified–
And carried Me away–

And now We roam in Sovreign Woods–
And now We hunt the Doe–
And every time I speak for Him–
The Mountains straight reply–

And do I smile, such cordial light
Upon the Valley glow–
It is as a Vesuvian face
Had let it's pleasure through–

And when at Night–Our good Day done–
I guard My Master's Head–
'Tis better than the Eider-Duck's
Deep Pillow–to have shared–

To foe of His–I'm deadly foe–
None stir the second time–
On whom I lay a Yellow Eye–
Or an emphatic Thumb–

Though I than He–may longer live
He longer must–than I–
For I have but the power to kill,
Without–the power to die–
                          (754, *about 1863*)

   5. in] the–
  16. Deep] low
  18. stir] harm
  23. power] art

The poem has no title. Thomas H. Johnson dates it about 1863 on the basis of her handwriting. In Ralph Franklin's recent facsimile edition of the forty fascicles as Dickinson arranged and bound them, this from the thirty-fourth, occurs ninth in a series of eighteen. The fact that ''My Life had stood–a Loaded Gun–'' is placed dead center may be chance or choice. It consists of six four-line stanzas loosely rhymed.[1] Written in the plain style of Puritan literary tradition, there are no complications of phrasing. Each word is deceptively simple, deceptively easy to define. But definition seeing rather than perceiving, hearing and not understanding, is only the shadow of meaning. Like all poems on the trace of the holy, this one remains outside the protection of specific solution. ''My Life had stood–a Loaded Gun–,'' written in a time of civil war, by a woman with little formal education in philosophy, carefully delineates and declines all aspects of the ''Will to Power'' nearly twenty years before Friedrich Nietzsche's metaphysical rebellion. Emily Dickinson's intellectual vigilance allowed very little to escape her without notice.

*   *   *

This is a frontier poem. Forester of New England wayward pilgrim. Trees have been stripped to the root by a seer on her path across circumference of intellection. This is a tragic poem. A pioneer's terse epic. Sorrow's melody is magic. Pitch of vowels, cadence of consonants, sound fused with sense–asceticism. For years I have wanted to find words to thank Emily Dickinson for the inspiration of her poetic daring. I hope by exploring the typology and topography of one singularly haunting work to make her extraordinary range perceptible to another reader.

---

1. Johnson breaks the lines into four per stanza, as Dickinson must have known would happen if they were ever printed. In her own handwriting the line-breaks are somewhat different. Although I have used the Johnson numbering for convenience, it should be remembered that she never numbered her poems. The Franklin edition is huge, Dickinson's handwriting is often difficult to decipher, and the book is extremely expensive. Few readers will have a chance to use it for reference, which is a pity, because it is necessary for a clearer understanding of her writing process.

Her, that dares be
What these lines wish to see;
I seek no further. it is She.
                    (Richard Crashaw,
    "Wishes to His Supposed Mistress")

    *   *   *

ARCHAEOLOGY

Foreshadowings:

I shall particularly speak of the severall Removes we had up and
down the Wilderness.

(Mary Rowlandson, *The Soveraignty & Goodnes of God*)

Emily Dickinson was born exactly two hundred years after the Great Migration led by John Winthrop brought her ancestors to America. Like Hawthorne, and unlike Emerson, her conscience still embraced the restless contradictions of this Puritan strain. Her ancestors, rigid Calvinists determined to walk the ancient ways and not to stumble on the path of Righteousness, voluntarily severed themselves from their origins to cross the northern ocean on a religious and utopian errand into the wilderness. Calvinism grounded in the Old Testament, through typological interpretation of the New, was an authoritarian theology that stressed personal salvation through strenuous morality, righteousness over love, and an autocratic governing principle over liberty. God's infinite and absolute sovereignty were conceived in terms of legal authority. Divine judgment and a moral law were necessary for a fallen humanity. Rage and rigor in the name of Jehovah, larded with threats and dire prophesies from the Books of Jeremiah and Hosea, required unswerving submission to HIS absolute dominion.

And *at what* instant I shall speak concerning a nation, and concerning a kingdom, to pluck up, and to pull down, and to destroy *it*;

Because my people hath forgotten me, they have burned incense to vanity, and they have caused them to stumble in their ways *from* the ancient paths, to walk in paths, *in* a way not cast up;

To make their land desolate, *and* a perpetual hissing; everyone that passeth thereby shall be astonished, and wag his head.

I will scatter them as with an east wind before the enemy; I will shew them the back, and not the face, in the day of their calamity.

(*Jeremiah*, 18:7, 15–17)

The vivid rhetoric of terror was a first step in the slow process toward American Democracy.

*   *   *

. . . –that man, being taught that he has nothing good left in his possession, and being surrounded on every side with the most miserable necessity, should, nevertheless, be instructed to aspire to the good of which he is destitute, and to the liberty of which he is deprived:

(Calvin, *Institutes*, II, ch. 2, i)

Calvinism aspiring to the good, of which man was destitute, soon banished any hint of liberalism in the Commonwealth. Cut off from familiar custom, from European civilization and its "enlightened" intellectual progression, trying to impose order on a real wilderness where winters were harsh, where wolves howled around the outskirts of each settlement, and a successful harvest often meant life or death to the community, the idea that our visible world is a whim and might be dissolved at any time hung on tenaciously. It was this profound conception of obedience to a stern and sovereign Absence that forged the fanatical energy necessary for survival. Obedience to a higher purpose warmed the physical and metaphysical loneliness of these pilgrim territories hugging the borders of an uncharted continent. In the beginning when life was precarious and therefore precious, each soul waited and prayed for the coming Millennium.

*   *   *

"I put for a general condition of all mankind a perpetual and restless desire of power after power, that ceaseth only in death." This Hobbesian notion dear to many Puritans, that every man in a primitive state of nature has the right to take what he can, led in one direction. The native Americans were robbed of their land, turned loose on each other, or exterminated. Antinomians, Separatists, and Quakers (often inspired and led by women) were summarily silenced, or driven from the borders of this modern Canaan.

*   *   *

That the Heathen People amongst whom we live, and whose Land the Lord God of our Fathers hath given to us for a rightful Possession, have at sundry times been Plotting mischievous Devices against that part of the *English Israel*, which is seated in these goings down of the Sun, no man that is an Inhabitant of any considerable standing, can be ignorant. Especially that there have been (*Nec Injuria*) Jealousies concerning the *Narragansets* and the *Wompanoags*, is notoriously known to all men.

(Increase Mather, *A History of the War*
with the Indians in New England, p. 46)

Hunting, fishing, and killing, were sacred occupations to the Indians. Along the New England coast different tribes, each united under a sachem or chief warrior, lived restlessly beside each other. The more peaceful Wampanoags in Massachusetts had long endured sporadic attacks from their neighbors the Narragansets. The war-like Pequots occupying the coast of Long Island Sound in Connecticut were hostile to Narragansets and to the Mohegans living in the central part of the area. Their tribes, long used to the eccentric rages and rewards of the unpredictable northern climate, and recently decimated by epidemic and famine, used Nature's providence sparingly. Survival in that vast expanse of wooded territory required spartan conditioning and tough preparedness from everyone. Frontier living changed the transplanted Puritan cavaliers in a variety of ways. Although most clung to a narrow, well-fortified fringe of cultivation along the eastern coast, increasingly members of the second generation felt they must go farther into the forest *with* the Indians. Frontiersmen and women stimulated by greed, and Chance, in this epic quest they had embarked on were eager to push farther west, exploring, farming, trapping, and trading. To dampen such dangerous individualism, the early Fathers of Massachusetts Bay, by using the colonists' love for the sermon as a field of action, cleverly manipulated the growing body of colonial writing.

"OH THOU SWORD of the wilderness, when wilt thou be quiet?"
(Cotton Mather, *Magnalia Christi americana*, Vol. 2, p. 639)

Visible saints and farmers on the edge of civilization, Indian captives, hunters, Indian fighters, missionaries–from their stories a national myth had been shaping itself. Narratives of conversion, discovery narratives, captivity and hunting stories, tales of the Pequot War and King Philip's War, blended with Indian place names, personal names, legend, and religion. Very often these separate visions had an expedition in common, and a sojourn in the wilderness. The early Defenders of the Faith, fearing more than anything else the marriage of English and American customs and beliefs, dwelt on the spell of this wooded place by concentrating on incidents of disappearance, murder, and cannibalism. The wilderness in subliminal and official Puritan myth stood as a microcosm for Mankind's fallen condition.

Cotton Mather's early Idealist conception of a "living and true God, infinite in being and perfection, a most pure spirit, immutable, immense, eternal, incomprehensible. . . . " degenerated under the unpredictable strains of frontier living into a jealous Sovereign, who would use any means to quell a hint of spiritual rebellion. Supernatural meddling explained natural phenomena. General providences became special providences.

> *June* 15. This day was seen at *Plimouth* the perfect form of an *Indian Bow* appearing in the aire, which the Inhabitants of that place . . . look upon, as a *Prodigious Apparition*. . . . Who knoweth but that it may be an *Omen* of ruine to the enemy, and that the Lord will break the bow and spear asunder, and make warrs to cease unto the ends of the earth?
>
> (Increase Mather, *History*, pp. 157–158)

*   *   *

> *Come, behold the works of the Lord, what dissolations he has made in the Earth*. Of thirty seven persons who were in this one House, none escaped either present death, or a bitter captivity, save only one, who might say as he. *Job 1.15. And I only am escaped alone to tell the News*. There were twelve killed, some shot, some stab'd with their Spears, some knock'd down with their Hatchets. When we are in prosperity, Oh the little that we think of such dreadfull sights, and to see our dear Friends, and Relations ly bleeding out their heart-blood upon the ground. There was one who was chopt into the head with a Hatchet, and stript naked, and yet was crawling up and down. It is a solemn sight to see so many Christians lying in their blood, some here, and some there, like a company of Sheep torn by Wolves. All of them stript naked by a company of hell-hounds, roaring, singing, ranting and insulting, as if they would have torn our very hearts out; yet the Lord by his Almighty power preserved a number of us from death, for there were twenty-four of us taken alive and carried Captive.
>
> (Mary Rowlandson, *Narrative*, pp. 4–5)

The Soveraignty and Goodnes of God, Together, With the Faithfulness of His Promises Displayed; Being a NARRATIVE of the Captivity and Restoration of Mrs. Mary Rowlandson. Commended by her, to all that desires to know the Lord's doings to and dealings with Her; was written by a Puritan woman to her "dear Children and Relations" as a reminder of God's providence, probably sometime in 1677, and was printed in Boston in 1682 after her death. This "True History" was enormously popular at once. Until the late eighteenth century captivity narratives dominated all other North American forms of frontier literature. Rowlandson's vivid account of the eleven weeks and five days she spent as a prisoner of the Narragansetts ushered in what was to become a major stream in American Mythology. At first the narratives were simple first-person accounts. As time went on and their popularity increased although generally narrated by woman, they were structured and written down by men. Richard Slotkin says in *Regeneration Through Violence*, that under Calvinist-Puritan control the stories were remarkably similar:

A WOMAN who has fallen into spiritual lethargy at home, is suddenly torn away from familiarity and family by marauding savages. During her captivity she suffers deprivation, humiliation, and terror. Time is no longer marked for her in minutes, hours, and days, but in a series of forced Removes, away from civilization deeper into the heart of the wilderness that is an emblem for Babylon. Survival depends on her ability to keep walking. She must never weaken or slow her captors down. She must learn to behave like an Indian woman, often serving an Indian Master. But survival as a Christian requires that she reject Indian marriage and participation, even if she is starving, in the pagan cannibal Eucharist. During her sojourn in Babylon she continues to read her Bible, particularly the Old Testament, and to beg the Lord's pardon for her own transgressions and those of her former neighbors. At last she transcends her situation by adapting to its exacting regimen. SHE who has been initiated into Wildness alone, now knows that affliction and initiation are violently One. She has learned to look beyond present troubles and can stand still with Moses and see the salvation of the Lord. Now SHE is ready for HIS inexorable determinism to effect her rescue and redemption.

Mary (White) Rowlandson's husband, Joseph, was a minister, and the only graduate of Harvard College in 1652. Sermons came to rely on each captive woman's suffering and deliverance. Her experience served as an apt metaphor for the process of Conversion.

*   *   *

Mythology reflects a region's reality. For many years the struggling Puritan communities did endure the fact and fantasy of Indian captivity. Villages worried and prayed over the strange behavior of returned captives, many of whom had been permanently altered by their experience. Hannah Dustin, a victim Cotton Mather particularly admired, had seen her newborn infant's brain splattered over the trunk of an apple tree. Later she and her nurse, Mary Neff, escaped by murdering several of their captors and scalping them for bounty. Captain Obediah Dickinson was among a group of soldiers taken captive in Deerfield, Massachusetts. He was forced to tie his friend to a stake and watch while the Indians tortured and burned him. Some victims had seen entire families slaughtered and scalped. Some had been forced to participate in ritual cannibalism. Most disturbing to first generation American Puritans were the captives, usually taken when they were children, who forgot their first language with their catechism, were adopted by and later married into loving Indian families, and in Canada, where they were usually taken, converted to a brand of French-Indian Catholicism. When these captives were found they often refused to come home.

The captives who were ransomed and "redeemed," knew what their neighbors dreaded to have thought. Puritanism was a Manichean religion. A Manichean Christian forced to subsist alone in the wild, was as prone to evil as any Heathen. Forceable initiation into Indian civilization showed the captives that the hardships their captors endured were often the result of English inroads on their land and the subsequent depletion of their food supplies. "I can remember the time, when I used to sleep quietly without workings in my thoughts, whole nights together, but now it is otherwayes with me," wrote Mary Rowlandson at the close of her narrative. She called it *The Soveraignty & Goodnes of GOD*, and she, or her husband, ended their Preface to the reader with Samson's riddle:

Out of the eater comes forth meat, and sweetness out of the strong.

*   *   *

MORE ENGLISH BLOOD SWALLOWED, BUT REVENGED.

                          (*Magnalia*, Vol. 2, p. 628)

July 19. Our Army pursued *Philip*, who fled unto a dismal Swamp
for refuge: The *English Souldiers* followed him, and killed many of his
men, also about fifteen of the *English* were then slain. The Swamp was
so Boggy, and thick of Bushes, as that it was judged to proceed further
therein would be but to throw away Mens lives. It could not there be
descerned who were *English*, and who the *Indians*. Our Men when in
that hideous place if they did but see a Bush stir would fire presantly,
whereby 'tis verily feared they did sometimes unhappily shoot *English
Men* instead of *Indians*.

(*History*, pp. 61-62)

Increase and Cotton Mather and their fellow Utopians had embarked on a sacred and irrational mission based on dread of the Irrational. The possibility of a marriage between English and native American cultures was anathema to these zealous Children of *Israel*. In the
desperate hunt for wilderness meat, an Elizabethan hunter-pilgrim desired and dreaded to become his own savage avatar.

*   *   *

For the present then the Indians have *done* murdering; they'll "do
so no more till next time." Let us then have *done* writing, when we
have a little informed our selves what is become of the chief murderers
among those wretches, for whom, if we could find a *name* of a length
like one of their own Indian long-winded words, it might be,
BOMBARDO-GLADIO-FUN-HASTI-FLAMMI-LOQUENTES.*

*Breathing, bombs, swords, death, spears, and flames.
(*Magnalia*, Vol. 2, p. 641)

*   *   *

I was in the Spirit on the Lord's day, and heard behind me a great
voice, as of a trumpet,
Saying, I am Alpha and Omega, the first and the last: and, What
thou seest, write in a book. . . .

(*Revelation*, 1:10-11)

On the Day of Revelation the holy city new Jerusalem will be
as a bride adorned for her husband. At the supper of the great God,
flesh of horses and flesh of humans will be eaten. The son of Man dressed

in a vestment dipped in blood will hold in his mouth a Sword that is the word of God. Jesus–"root and offspring of David, and the bright and morning star"–Lucifer.

From the first, New England legend and myth, based on rigid separation of race, concentrated on abduction, communion, war, and diabolism. Contradiction is the book of this place.

*   *   *

MY LIGHT IS MY DEATH

Mercenary and racist as it soon became, originally this had been a plantation of religion. John Cotton, Cotton and Increase Mather, Thomas Hooker, Michael Wigglesworth, Thomas Shephard, finally and most interestingly, Jonathan Edwards; the Calvinist theocracy produced brilliant, idealistic intellects. Most broke down in some way under the strain of worldly ambition that clashed with morbid fear and merciless introspection. Naked and alone each unquiet heart waited to learn God's sovereign and arbitrary Plan. Everlasting damnation or the slim chance of election to salvation waited beyond an unseen Ocean.

> I know not how to express better what my sins appear to me to be, than by heaping infinite upon infinite, and multiplying infinite by infinite. Very often, for these many years, these expressions are in my mind, and in my mouth, "Infinite upon infinite . . . Infinite upon infinite!" When I look into my heart, and take a view of my wickedness, it looks like an abyss infinitely deeper than hell. And it appears to me, that were it not for free grace, exhalted and raised up to the infinite height of all the fulness and glory of the great Jehova, and the arm of his power and grace stretched forth in all the majesty of his power, and all the glory of his sovereignty, I should appear sunk down in my sins below hell itself; far beyond the sight of every thing, but the eye of sovereign grace, that can pierce even down to such a depth.
>
> (Jonathan Edwards, "Personal Narrative," pp. 70–71)

Dualism of visible and invisible. This turning in of the Puritan on himself, this humiliation and self-examination, had its opposite momentum toward contemplation and peace. In the Valley of the Shadow of Death I may see the irrational beauty of life.

God's excellency, his wisdom, his purity and love, seemed to appear
in every thing; in the sun, moon, and stars; in the clouds, and blue
sky; in the grass, flowers, trees; in the water, and all nature; which
used greatly to fix my mind. I often used to sit and view the moon
for continuance; and in the day, spent much time in viewing the clouds
and sky, to behold the sweet glory of God in these things; in the mean
time, singing forth, with a low voice my contemplations of the Creator
and Redeemer. . . . Before, I used to be uncommonly terrified with
thunder, and to be struck with terror when I saw a thunder storm rising; but now, on the contrary, it rejoiced me.

> ("Personal Narrative," pp. 60–61)

Not to set forth my Self, but to lose and find it in diligent search.
Obedience and submission to one will, was the journey of return to
the sacred source human frailty had lost. Puritan theology at its best
would tirelessly search God's secrecy, explore Nature's hidden meaning.

*   *   *

GUNS AND GRACE

Calvinist religious introspection found fear and fascinated loathing
in the daemonic energy of Satan. Counter to diabolical force was the
gift of Grace granted by God to some of his children. Great sins drew
out great grace, said John Bunyan in *Grace Abounding*. The Kingdom
of Heaven might be reached through confession of sin, repentance,
renunciation, and righteousness. Conversion and regeneration of each
member of every congregation depended on this. A struggling community at the edge of mapped earth, whose citizens too often witnessed
the malevolent power in nature, couldn't at first tolerate the chaos of
a mystical vision of grace as free imaginative force. To quell real terror, they must discipline nature, smother the arbitrary power of Jehovah
with a Covenant.

Whereas the opinions and revelations of Mr. Wheelwright and Mrs.
Hutchinson have seduced and led into dangerous errors many of the
people here in New England, insomuch as there is just cause of suspicion that they, as others in Germany, in former times, nay, upon some
revelation, make some sudden eruption upon those that differ from them

in judgement, for prevention whereof it is ordered, that all those whose names are underwritten shall (upon warning given or left at their dwelling houses) before the 30th of this month of November, deliver at Mr. Cane's house at Boston, all such guns, pistols, swords, powder, shot, and match as they shall be owners of, or have in their custody, upon pain of ten pounds for every default. . . .

                                        (*Massachusetts Records*.I, pp. 211–12)

The gift of grace was never for sale. Grace caused a civil war in the Calvinist soul. Grace often visited the elect, with visionary intensity born in ecstasy and trance. Domain of creative immediacy and intellectual beauty, awakened before the finite front of time, Pilgrim arrives as in a dream. On this enchanted ground, weary of similitudes, weary of law, I might withdraw into distance beyond name.

The concept of Predestination presupposes that I am morally loathesome, abominable to HIS vision. Grace and Predestination are another contradiction, or so it must have seemed to Anne Hutchinson. To Jonathan Edwards as late as 1740, the contradiction was compatible, proved by the scientific discoveries of Sir Isaac Newton, and John Locke's *Essay Concerning Human Understanding*.

                    *   *   *

CONVERSANT WITH SPIDERS

The Puritan consciousness of Jonathan Edwards (1703–1758) shadows and prefigures that of Emily Dickinson. Edwards's famous ministry was in Northampton, and Amherst was a neighboring village. During the first half of the eighteenth century, Northampton, still a frontier community, was the most influential ecclesiastical region in the Connecticut River Valley. Edwards' wide learning, his dynamic preaching, and his writing placed him at the center of the Great Religious Awakening of the late 1730s and '40s. In several tracts, the most important being "A Faithful Narrative of the Surprising Work of God," and "Thoughts of the Revival in New England," he carefully documented the remarkable religious frenzy of that time and his own part in lighting the match to emotions that swiftly kindled into flame. These tracts later became basic texts for revivalist preaching in America, Scot-

land, and England and were widely read and used well into the nineteenth century. His *Complete Works*, edited by S. Austin, were published in 1808, and reprinted in four volumes in 1844 and 1847. In
1855 Samuel Bowles published Josiah Gilbert Holland's *History of Western
Massachusetts*. Both men were close friends of the Dickinson family; Emily
Dickinson was particularly close to them. Holland, who knew Edwards'
writing well and the influence his thinking had exerted on their region,
called him "a metaphysician and theologian second to none in America."
In fact Edwards was far more than a ranting Calvinist preacher of hellfire
and damnation; he was the most astute and original American philosopher to write before the age of James, Peirce, and Santayana.

*   *   *

Jonathan Edwards' apocalyptic sermons voice human terror of oblit-
eration in our lonely and inexplicable cosmos. He exhorts us to turn
from the world, to live ascetically, while actively striving to obtain
the emotional peace that is grace. Calvinist doctrine, as interpreted by
this Neoplatonist inheritor of a lost cause in America, found no path
to eternal life through material success. It forbade retreat and monastic
isolation, at the same time emphasizing "Justification by faith alone" –
another contradiction. Each person's active participation was called for
in the battle against sin. To be in the world but avoid serving Mam-
mon, I must renounce attachment to friends and worldly accomplish-
ment. Recognition by the world is not recognition by God, and is
therefore a delusion. Worry and regret over lack of recognition are empty
and a snare.

To T.W. Higginson   *7 June 1862*

I smile when you suggest that I delay "to publish"–that being
foreign to my thought, as Firmament to Fin–
If fame belonged to me, I could not escape her–if she did not, the
longest day would pass me on the chase–and the approbation of my
Dog, would forsake me–then–My Barefoot-Rank is better–

(L265)

Emily Dickinson's religion was Poetry. As she went on through
veils of connection to the secret alchemy of Deity, she was less and

less interested in temporal blessing. The decision not to publish her
poems in her lifetime, to close up an extraordinary amount of work,
is astonishing. Far from being the misguided modesty of an oppressed
female ego, it is a consummate Calvinist gesture of self-assertion by
a poet with faith to fling election loose across the incandescent shadows
of futurity.

*   *   *

Had renunciation and clarity of imagery been all Edward's
theological writing offered Dickinson, she might have passed him by.
Purity of motive and holy idealism can be found in many places. She
found them in Shelley's *Defense of Poetry*, in Browning's "Shelley and
the Art of Poetry," possibly in Ruskin's writing about Turner's paint-
ing, certainly in Thoreau's *Walden*, and in Emerson's poems and lec-
tures. But Edwards' negativity, his disciplined journey through con-
scious despair, humiliation, and the joy of submission to an arbitrary
and absent ordering of the Universe, presaged hers.

These two prophets of American Modernism speculated in a
linguistic territory of ferocious morality. There, mystical revelation col-
lided with self-tormenting literalism. Ascension has a muffled route,
fidelity never flickers—with the awe of startled children they listened
even to the sleeping rocks dreaming.

> Contained in this short Life
> Are magical extents
> The soul returning soft at night
> To steal securer thence
> As Children strictest kept
> Turn soonest to the sea
> Whose nameless Fathoms slink away
> Beside infinity
>
> (1165)

*   *   *

John Locke's Essay *Concerning Human Understanding* helped to form
Edwards's conviction, and one quite relevant to Dickinson's writing
process, that words are annexed to reality by sensation, facts charged

with meaning by an intelligence behind them. In Book III of "The Essay" Locke supplied him with an idea of the Universe as organized around the act of perception. If language imposes on the understanding names which familiarity has deadened, how does a minister preach a sermon when words and images have become predictable? Ideas must be stripped to their essence, rhetorical embroidery torn off.

> Then since within this wide great *Vniuerse*
> Nothing doth firme and permanent appeare,
> But all things tost and turned by transuerse:
> What then should let, but I aloft should reare
> My Trophee, and from all, the triumph beare?
> (Edmund Spenser, *The Faerie Queene,*
> "Mutabilitie," VII, 56)

One hundred and forty years after the death of Spenser, Newton had gone farther than Copernicus in assaulting the Ptolemaic paradigm of an ordered Universe. Edwards saw, as other American intellectuals of his time did not, that the customary Ramist rhetoric must be jettisoned along with the old physics. Human dislocation and terror of uncertainty in a rapidly changing social system and cosmos must be spoken in a new tongue. His apocalyptic sermons locate his listeners alone on an inscape of force.

The God that holds you over the pit of hell, much as one holds a spider, or some loathsome insect over the fire, abhors you, and is dreadfully provoked: his wrath towards you burns like fire; he looks upon you as worthy of nothing else, but to be cast into the fire; he is of purer eyes than to bear to have you in his sight; you are ten thousand times more abominable in his eyes, than the most hateful venomous serpent is in ours. You have offended him infinitely more than ever a stubborn rebel did his prince; and yet it is nothing but his hand that holds you from falling into the fire every moment. It is to be ascribed to nothing else, that you did not go to hell last night that you was suffered to awake again in this world, after you closed your eyes to sleep.
(Edwards, "Sinners in the Hands of an Angry God," p. 164)

Perry Miller said that Jonathan Edwards' understanding of behavioral psychology, as evidenced by his careful documentation of the process of Conversion, anticipates American empiricism and William James. I say that Emily Dickinson took both his legend and his learning, tore them free from his own humorlessness and the dead weight of doctrinaire Calvinism, then applied the freshness of his perception to the dead weight of American poetry as she knew it.

> We met as Sparks–Diverging Flints
> Sent various–scattered ways–
> We parted as the Central Flint–
> Were cloven with an Adze–
> Subsisting on the Light We bore
> Before We felt the Dark–
> We knew by change between itself
> And that etherial Spark.
>
> (958)
>
> 7–8] A Flint unto this Day–perhaps–
> But for that single Spark.

Edwards's stark presentation of the immanent consciousness of Separation enters the structure of her poems. Each word is a cipher, through its sensible sign another sign hidden. The recipient of a letter, or combination of letter and poem from Emily Dickinson, was forced much like Edwards' listening congregation, through shock and through subtraction of the ordinary, to a new way of perceiving. Subject and object were fused at that moment, into the immediate *feeling* of understanding. This re-ordering of the forward process of reading is what makes her poetry and the prose of her letters among the most original writing of her century.

To T.W. Higginson *August 1880*

Dear Friend,

I was touchingly reminded of your little Louisa this Morning by an Indian Woman with gay Baskets and a dazzling Baby, at the Kitchen Door–Her little Boy ''once died,'' she said, Death to her dispelling him–I asked her what the Baby liked, and she said ''to step.'' The Prairie before the Door was gay with Flowers of Hay, and I led her in–She argued with the Birds–she leaned on Clover Walls and they fell, and dropped her–With jargon sweeter than a Bell, she grappled

Buttercups – and they sank together, the Buttercups the heaviest – What
sweetest use of Days!

'Twas noting some such Scene made Vaughn humbly say "My
Days that are at best but dim and hoary" –

I think it was Vaughn –

It reminded me too of "Little Annie," of whom you feared to make
the mistake in saying "Shoulder Arms" to the "Colored Regiment" – but
which was the Child of Fiction, the Child of Fiction or of Fact, and
is "Come unto me" for Father or Child, when the Child precedes?

(L653)

*   *   *

In 1750 Jonathan Edwards was dismissed by his congregation and
banished by circumstance and choice to Stockbridge, Massachusetts.
At the time, Stockbridge, beyond the line of frontier, was wilderness.
The village consisted of twelve white families who disliked him before
he arrived, and two hundred and fifty quarrelling Indians from the
Mohawk and Housatunnock tribes. It was a community in constant
tension from within and without. Here in a primitive log meeting house,
one of the only philosophers America has ever managed to produce,
and certainly the greatest intellect in New England at the time, preached
to a meager and disgruntled Indian audience on the evils of alcoholism
and stealing. In the privacy of a tiny study, at the edge of European
civilization, this unyielding, isolate, searcher, who had never travelled
farther than Boston, had never seen a cathedral or a castle, this mystical
empiricist and belated interpreter of Calvin, wrote "The Nature of True
Virtue," "Freedom of the Will," and "Concerning the End for which
God created the World."

*   *   *

Jonathan Edwards carefully sewed his work into handsome note-
books, as did Emily Dickinson. Among his manuscripts are several con-
taining 212 numbered entries he made with different inks and pens over
the span of his life. Miscellanies-fragments; like her poems they were
never meant for publication. They have since been published under the
titles *Images and Shadows of Divine Things,* and *The Beauty of the World.*

*   *   *

THE DISTANCE BETWEEN TWO

1723] When Jonathan Edwards was twenty, he met thirteen-year-old Sarah Pierrepont while on a visit to New Haven. The young and very serious theological student, who had grown up an only brother, fifth in order of birth, among eleven sisters, wrote this lyrical portrait of his future wife, on the blank page of a book he was reading.

> They say there is a young lady in [New Haven] who is beloved of that Great Being, who made and rules the world, and that there are certain seasons in which this Great Being, in some way or other invisible, comes to her and fills her mind with exceeding sweet delight, and that she hardly cares for any thing, except to meditate on him–that she expects after a while to be received up where he is, to be raised up out of the world and caught up into heaven; being assured that he loves her too well to let her remain at a distance from him always. There she is to dwell with him, and to be ravished with his love and delight forever. Therefore, if you present all the world before her, with the richest of its treasures, she disregards it and cares not for it, and is unmindful of any pain or affliction. She has a strange sweetness in her mind, and singular purity in her affections; is most just and conscientious in all her conduct; and you could not persuade her to do any thing wrong or sinful, if you would give her all the world, lest she should offend this Great Being. She is of a wonderful sweetness, calmness, and universal benevolence of mind; especially after this Great God has manifested himself to her mind. She will sometimes go about from place to place, singing sweetly; and seems to be always full of joy and pleasure; and no one knows for what. She loves to be alone, walking in the fields and groves, and seems to have someone invisible always conversing with her.

> (Edwards, "Sarah Pierrepont," p. 56)

1750] Among Edwards's posthumous papers, is a rough draft of his farewell letter to the Congregation in Northampton that had so roughly dismissed him. He had been their minister for twenty-three years. The final sentence reads:

> I am dear brethren He who was your *affectionate* and I hope through grace faithful pastoral servant for Jesus sake.

> J.E.

The word *affectionate* has been carefully crossed out.

*   *   *

1846]   Emily Dickinson's Western Massachusetts was a very different place from the small community of hardy fractious traders, trap-
pers, and farmers Edwards had preached to a hundred years earlier. An
old idea of rugged defensiveness had broken apart in its own contradictions. Only its dim reflection was seen in the surface community of
towns like Amherst, where polite Victorian respectability and the oc-
casional excitement of another religious revival capped the slow dissolu-
tion of an agrarian community in the process of rapid economic and
industrial transformation. During Emily Dickinson's lifetime the railroad
came to Amherst. Boston and New York were easy trips away and
many of her friends travelled to Europe or California. She remained
at home. In a letter to Abiah Root written when she was sixteen, she
quoted these lines from Edward Young:

> With how much emphasis the poet has said, "We take no note
> of Time, but from its loss. T'were wise in man to give it then a tongue.
> Pay no moment but in just purchase of it's worth & what it's worth,
> ask death beds. They can tell. Part with it as with life reluctantly."
>
> (L13)

Already worrying about the metaphysical puzzle of time, she knew
by instinct what most of us take years to learn, that time lived forward
is only understood backward, that social existence merely negates spiritual
progress. Dickinson's refusal during her teens to join the Congrega-
tional Church during the Great Awakening that swept the region once
again left her startlingly alone. Dislocation first rends the seeking soul.
Splendor is subversive to the Collective will. In the eye of the present,
fragments of past presents. My presence keeps a promise to past meanings. Emily Dickinson's refusal to bend under great community pressure
recalls the stubborn strength in isolation of Mary Rowlandson. Her
intuitive spiritual apprehension links her with Anne Hutchinson and
Mary Dyer. As one intelligence conversant with the best thought of
another, she is Jonathan Edwards's enlightened successor.

*   *   *

1851]   When she was twenty-one Emily Dickinson gaily sent her
brother Austin this account of a Dickinson family excursion to hear
a famous singer perform in Northampton.

6 July

-what words express our horror when rain began to fall-in drops-
sheets-cataracts-what *fancy conceive* of drippings and of drenchings which
we met on the way-how the stage and its mourning captives drew up
at Warner's hotel-how all of us alighted, and were conducted in, how
the rain did not abate, how we walked in silence to the old Edwards
Church and took our seats in the same, how Jennie came out like a
child and sang and sang again, how boquets fell in showers, and the
roof was rent with applause-how it thundered outside, and inside with
the thunder of God and of men-judge ye which was the loudest-how
we all loved Jennie Lind, but not accustomed oft to her manner of singing
didn't fancy *that* so well as we did *her*-no doubt it was very fine-but
take some notes from her "Echo"-the Bird sounds from the "Bird
Song" and some of her curious trills, and I'd rather have a Yankee.

(L46)

Jenny Lind is the only professional singer or musician that Emily
Dickinson is known to have heard perform.

Sound was always part of perfect meaning. A young poet listens
to Jenny Lind singing bird sounds from the "Bird Song" in the old
church where a century earlier a last Puritan minister and first American
philosopher spoke the word of God to his congregation, "unto the
three and twentieth year, rising early and speaking." Complex cor-
respondences exist and kindred definitions. Unknown harbinger of sen-
suous phenomena, Sound has come to us unknown. "Inside the civilized
man stands the savage still in the place of honor," wrote Thoreau in
A Week on the Concord and Merrimack Rivers, nine years after Emily
Dickinson was born. In his transcendent autumnal meditation on Time,
he returns again and again to the severe poetry of our early History.
Pursuit and possession. Through a forest of mystic meaning, Religion
hunts for Poetry's freedom, while Poetry roams Divinity's sovereign
source.

*   *   *

1881]   A Little Boy ran away from Amherst a few Days ago, and
when asked where he was going, replied, "Vermont or Asia."
Many of us go farther. My pathetic Crusoe– . . .
          Vails of Kamtchatka dim the Rose–in my Puritan Garden,
and as a farther stimulus, I had an Eclipse of the Sun a few Morn-
ings ago, but every Crape is charmed–
          I knew a Bird that would sing as firm in the centre of Dissolu-
tion, as in it's Father's nest–
Phenix, or the Robin?

                                                                    (L685)

                    *   *   *

1881]   This note accompanied a dead bee.

          For Gilbert to carry to his Teacher–

                    The Bumble Bee's Religion–

                    His little Hearse like Figure
                    Unto itself a Dirge
                    To a delusive Lilac
                    The vanity divulge
                    Of Industry and Morals
                    And every righteous thing
                    For the divine Perdition
                    Of Idleness and Spring–

          "All Liars shall have their part"–
          Jonathan Edwards–
          "And let him that is athirst come"–
          Jesus–
                                        (L712)

                    *   *   *

1715]   Nor Can any one Go out amongst the trees in a Dewey morning
towards the latter end of august or at the beginning of september
but that he shall see hundreds of webbs made Conspicuous by
the Dew that is lodged upon them reaching from one tree & shrub
to another that stand at a Considerable Distance, and they may
be seen well enough by an observing eye at noon Day by their
Glistening against the sun and what is still more wonderfull: i

know I have severall times seen in a very Calm and serene Day
at that time of year, standing behind some Opake body that shall
just hide the Disk of the sun and keep of his Dazzling rays from
my eye and looking close by the side of it, multitudes of little
shining webbs and Glistening Strings of a Great Length and at
such a height as that one would think they were tack'd to the
Sky . . . and there Very Often appears at the end of these Webs
a Spider floating and sailing in the air with them

(Edwards, "Of Insects," p. 3)

*   *   *

To Imagination

September 3, 1844

So hopeless is the world without,
The world within I doubly prize;
Thy world where guile and hate and doubt
And cold suspicion never rise;
Where thou and I and Liberty
Have undisputed sovereignty.

(Emily Brontë)

After the age of twenty, having meantime studied alone with diligence and perseverance, she went with me to an establishment on the Continent. The same suffering and conflict ensued, heightened by the strong recoil of her upright, heretic and English spirit from the gentle Jesuitry of the foreign and Romish system.

(Charlotte Brontë, Extract from the "Prefatory Note" to *Selections from Poems by Ellis Bell*.)

ENGLAND AND NEW ENGLAND, to Jonathan Edwards, "this Nation" . . . Across an ocean the brief lives of the Brontës and their legend touched hers. Emily Brontë died in 1848 when Emily Dickinson was eighteen, Anne in 1849, and Charlotte, who married in 1854, died of complications due to pregnancy a year later. These three clever, articulate sisters were geographically cut off from the intellectual world they were in literary contact with, as was Dickinson. Childhood had subjected them to an austere Calvinism, through its descendent, evangelical Methodism, that left its mark in emotional ambivalence like hers. The Brontës were the daughters of an Anglican clergyman of Irish extraction; their mother died of cancer after bearing six children in seven years of marriage. Of the four surviving children, only Charlotte had even a vague memory of her. Dickinson was the daughter of a stern and patriarchal lawyer, whose wife seems to have been nervous, sickly, and ineffectual. Mothers played an insignificant role in all of their upbringing. Their own status as adult women, who were spinsters in provincial towns, where each family was considered superior, and where they were expected to behave with a required feminine decorum they had little interest in, was a paradox. They suffered the tormenting paralysis of women deadlocked by a culture that treated them as both servant and superior. Dickinson was rich, the Brontës poor, but their options, limited by class and sex, were relatively similar. The Brontës also had an adored and troubled brother, on whose insecure shoulders the hopes of his sisters rested. Although Branwell's life was a public disaster, provincial Yorkshire was not so easily shocked by eccentric behavior. Austin Dickinson's self-destructiveness was more discreet. Eventually his marital infidelity caused a suppressed scandal in Amherst. The New England code required that such "shame" be silenced. Suppressed shame like Blake's Poison Tree, watered with fears and deceit, bears poison fruit. The wounds to a clear understanding of the strength of his sister Emily's character, to say nothing of the willful mutilation of her papers, were the direct result of his and his inheritors' obsession with their own propriety.

       *   *   *

My sister Emily loved the moors. Flowers brighter than the rose
bloomed in the blackest of the heath for her; out of a sullen hollow in a
livid hill-side her mind could make an Eden. She found in the bleak solitude many and dear delights; and not the least and best loved was–liberty.
(Charlotte Brontë, "Memoir of Emily Jane Brontë," p. 22)

Of the three Brontë sisters, Emily was both recluse and visionary.
A close reading of her life and work is crucial for understanding Emily
Dickinson. Out of Brontë's Self, out of her Myth, the younger woman
chose to pull her purity of purpose. Metamorphosis of thought into
corresponding vocation, Myself was as another, now "I" dare to go
farther.

> Bereavement in their death to feel
> Whom We have never seen–
> A Vital Kinsmanship import
> Our Soul and their's–between–
>
> For Stranger–Strangers do not mourn–
> There be Immortal friends
> Whom Death see first–'tis news of this
> That paralyze Ourselves–
>
> Who, vital only to Our Thought–
> Such Presence bear away
> In dying–'tis as if Our Souls
> Absconded–suddenly–
>
> (645)
> The first poem in fascicle 34.
> 11. Souls] World–/Selves–/Sun–

In the separate souls of these two women, once again the inhuman
legalism of Calvin warred with the intellectual beauty of Neoplatonism.
Violence of the occult in puritan thought. Twofold wisdom, rational
and supernatural–ceaseless mythic advance of poetic composition. I call
Wuthering Heights a poem.

*   *   *

If God created Man and Woman to damn them, Emily Brontë
sided with the sinners and was recalcitrant. In the fictional-real world

of Gondal, in the doomed defiant oneness of Heathcliff and Catherine, she dismembered the surface cohesion of Mind's civilization. Society, a hostile territory, would always force passion that was infinite to conform to finite necessity.

> Nature is an inexplicable puzzle, life exists on a principle of destruction; every creature must be the relentless instrument of death to the others, or himself cease to live. Nevertheless, we celebrate the day of our birth, and we praise God that we entered such a world. In the course of my soliloquy I picked a flower at my side. It was pretty and newly opened, but an ugly caterpillar had hidden himself among the petals and already they were drawing up and withering. "Sad image of the earth and its inhabitants!" I exlaimed, "This worm lives only by destroying the plant which protects him; why was he created and why was man created? He torments, he kills, he devours; he suffers, dies, is devoured–that's his whole story. It is true that there is a heaven for the saint, but the saint leaves enough misery here below to sadden him even before the throne of God."
> I threw the flower to the ground; at that moment the universe appeared to me a vast machine constructed only to bring forth evil.
> (Emily Brontë, "The Butterfly,"
> Five Essays Written in French, p. 17)

At times the entire universe was hostile, and love a force in nature exactly equivalent to hate. Away from her home in Yorkshire, prevented by poverty from turning with pleasure into the liberty solitude offered, Emily Brontë found it hard to believe in a God of justice and mercy.

> Speaking theologically–pay heed, for I rarely speak as a theologian–it was God himself who at the end of his labour lay down as a serpent under the Tree of Knowledge: it was thus he recuperated from being God . . . He had made everything too beautiful . . . The Devil is merely the idleness of God on that seventh day . . .
> (Nietzsche, Ecco Home, "Beyond Good and Evil" p. 113)

Emily Brontë and Emily Dickinson, two of the self-emancipated "little women" Nietzsche was so fond of scorning, often anticipate him in their writing.

*   *   *

"Honor thy father and thy mother—if thou wilt live." In such a commandment God reveals the baseness of man in His sight; for human beings to perform the tenderest and holiest of all duties, a threat is necessary; through fear He must force a blessing on the maniac. In this commandment is hidden a reproach bitterer than any open accusation could express; a charge of total blindness or of infernal ingratitude.

Parents love their children, that is a law of nature; the hind does not fear the hounds when her young is in danger, the bird dies on its nest; this instinct is a spark of the divine soul which we share with every living creature, and has God not put in the heart of the child a similar feeling? Something of that feeling undoubtedly exists, and yet the voice of thunder cries to them: "Honor thy parents or thou shalt die!"

("Filial Love," p. 13)

This author, essentially anonymous, walks in her imagination satanically to and fro up and down in Job's primal world of God's Plan. Sum and comprehension of perfection and desolation, all eclipses and real existences are one Imagination. Seductive compulsion to rest. Born posthumously I will pass through death into infinite peace under the soil of finite earth. All will, all human striving, must be oriented toward re-establishing in Death the lost harmony of Ideal beauty. Affirmation in negation, all motion, all direction is toward *this* pedestination. One wrong step may subvert right purpose.

His courage is not temerity, nor is his pride arrogance. His anger is justified, his assurance is free from presumption. He has an inner conviction that by no mortal victory will he be defeated. Death alone can gain victory over his arms. To her he is ready to yield, for Death's touch is to the hero what the striking off his chains is to the slave.

("King Harold on the Eve of the Battle of Hastings," p. 12)

Emily Jane Brontë died of consumption when she was only thirty. The calendar called it Tuesday, the 19th of December, 1848 . . . birth of the Festival of Winter. On Monday the 18th, Charlotte had read to her from Emerson's essays " . . . I read on till I found she was not listening."

*　　　　*　　　　*

Henry Adams to Charles Francis Adams, Jr.   *London. 14 May 1863.*

He went on in his thoughtful, deliberative, way, addressing Browning.

"Do you think your success would be very much more valuable to you for knowing that centuries hence, you would still be remembered? Do you look to the future connection by a portion of mankind, of certain ideas with your name, as the great reward of all your labour?

"Not in the least! I am perfectly indifferent whether my name is remembered or not. The reward would be that the ideas which were mine, should live and benefit the race! . . .

"Well, now Browning, suppose you, some time or other, were to meet Shakespeare, as perhaps some of us may. You would rush to him, and seize his hand, and cry out, 'dear Shakespeare, how delighted I am to see you. You can't imagine how much they think and talk about you on earth!' Do you suppose Shakespeare would be more carried away by such an announcement than I should be at hearing that I was remembered by the boys at Mother S's at Fulham? What possible advantage can it be to him to know that what he did on earth is still remembered there?"

The same idea is in LXIII of Tennyson's *In Memoriam*, but not pointed the same way. It was curious to see the two men who, of all others, write for fame, or have done so, ridicule the idea of its real value to them.

But Browning went on to get into a very unorthodox humor, and developed a theory of spiritual election that would shock the Pope, I fear. According to him, the minds or souls that really did develop themselves and educate themselves in life, could alone expect to enter a future career for which this life was a preparatory course. The great were rejected, turned back, God knows what becomes of them; these myriads of savages and brutalized and degraded Christians. Only those that could pass the examination were allowed to commence the new career. This is Calvin's theory, modified; and really it seems not unlikely to me. Thus this earth may serve as a sort of feeder to the next world, as the lower and middle classes here do to the aristocracy, here and there furnishing a member to fill the gaps. The corollaries of this proposition are amusing to work out.

(*The Letters of H. Adams*, vol. I, pp. 354–355)

*   *   *

Emily: Feminine of the Teutonic Emil, "the industrious," stems from Amalia of the ancient Goths; and Amalia, or Amelia, goes back to the wild forest people known as the Ameler.

* * *

Peace is a fiction of our Faith—
The Bells a Winter Night
Bearing the Neighbor out of Sound
That never did alight.

(912)

4. alight] delight

* * *

Part Three

TRUMPETS SING TO BATTLE

"CHILDE ROLAND TO THE DARK TOWER CAME"
(See Edgar's Song in "LEAR"
Robert Browning, "Childe Roland," Title)

Glou.   No words, no words: Hush
Edg.   Childe Rowland to the dark tower came;
        His word was still,–Fie, foh, and fum,
        I smell the blood of a British man.[a]
                        (Shakespeare, *King Lear*, III, iv, 178–181)

a) Capell has an ingenious note to show that Childe Rowland was the
Knight Orlando; that the lines are part of an old ballad, of which one
line has been accidentally omitted; and that we should read–

> "Childe Rowland to the dark tower come,
> *The giant roar'd, and out he ran;*
> His word was still–Fie, foh, and fum,
> I smell the blood of a British man."
>   (footnote to Knight's *The Comedies, Histories,*
>   *Tragedies, and Poems of W. Shakespeare,* 1853.
>   Dickinson and Browning both knew this
>   edited version.)

One of the strangest passages in *King Lear*–even the Arden edition footnotes are at a loss to locate any one source for Shakespeare
here. The little babble-song sung by sane-mad Edgar-Tom to Gloucester,
his father, who hears but doesn't know him, first recalls Charlemagne's
Roland, and through him, bravery, self-sacrifice and chivalry. Second,
Jack the giant Killer, through him the nursery. Finally, when mythic
Helen was carried away by a sea monster, her brother Childe Roland
crossed the sea in search of her. She hid him while the monster was
gone; when he returned he smelled the blood of a Christian man.

What dark tower? Why did Robert Browning structure his enigmatic poem around this one line, then direct his readers to the rest
of Edgar's mad song? Both "Childe Roland to the Dark Tower Came"
and "My Life had stood–a Loaded Gun–," written in the latter half
of the nineteenth century, are triumphantly negative poems. Their
authors, alien explicators of ruin after the Tablets of the Law were
broken, live on in archaic time beyond future. At the end of each poem,

austere originators have unselved identity, memory, poetic origins–
Originality. Each lyrical "I," liberated from individual will, will die
into action.

Two nameless narrators in the middle of life were set on their path
to the questionable freedom of paralysis in power by a nameless, vaguely
threatening Guide/Owner. Exiles, they wander a wilderness of language
formed from old legends, precursor poems, archaic words, industrial
and literary detritus. Cynical and gleefully aggressive, these travellers
now know that Beauty is allied to Blasphemy, and Danger, a wise interpreter. Here is *Pilgrim's Progress* and Pilgrim isn't Christian. In this
predatory old/New World of hunter and hunted, communal identity
has been lost, time lost, specificity of place lost, sure belief lost, purpose lost. These wayfarers are free–too free. Outside, alert estray. . . .
Only a sublime and sovereign sun kindles and dives malevolently down.
Night has come. The lure-dark Tower, blind as the fool's heart was
a squat mirage too late. At the edge of unknown, the sacred inaccessible unseen–Lyric "I" is both guard and hunter. *We* and *We* prey
on each other. Absence is the admired presence of each poem. Death
roams the division–World's november. Two separate Questors have
found nothing but noise of their own aggressive monologues echoing.
Firm allegory has escaped into the heart of human cruelty, Love's unfa-
thomable mystery. Into the desolate attraction of annihilation, dauntless
they will turn and turn again telling.

                    *   *   *

"Because I could not stop for Death" (712), and "My life had
stood–a Loaded Gun–" (754), were probably written around 1863.
The debt that the first of these two great poems owes to Robert Browning's "The Last Ride Together" has already been established. When
the poems are put beside each other, the similarities are obvious. With
a few images from *Aurora Leigh*, and her own wit and terse urgency,
Dickinson re-wrote his poem. Changing Browning's "Mistress" to
her "Master," Death, she wrote an American woman's version. "The
Last Ride Together," "Childe Roland," "By the Fireside," "Love
among the Ruins," and "Memorabilia," were all published in Browning's collection *Men and Women*, in 1855. Dickinson, of all people,

would have read "Childe Roland" as a poem of anxiety over poetic origins. It was indebted in turn, to Elizabeth Barrett's earlier and far weaker "A Vision of Poets," 1844. Dickinson had already responded to that poem with "I died for Beauty" (449) in 1862. In this case she would have heeded Browning's specific instruction to "see Edgar's Song in LEAR."

*   *   *

Dickinson and Browning were both instinctive masters of the art of dramatic Monologue. Their secretive natures knew soliloquy's power to conceal as it reveals messages. Anonymous shape-changer, she carried the concealing farther. Her poems are monologues without a named narrator, their supreme source is Shakespeare. *Lear* is a play charged with linguistic energy, dissimulation, consecration, invocation, quibble, sleight-of-hand, and illusion; constant reversals of meaning, constant wordplay on "seeing" and "nothing". The good, Kent and Edgar, must resort to exile, disguise, and cunning, while Edmund, the villain, is witty, attractive, and beguiling. LEAR dark pastoral. Men and women thrust out of Society, find desolation, destruction, and renewal in the mystic forest of the heart. The fleeing of absolute love beyond the borders of death into Myth is the progress of *King Lear, Wuthering Heights*, and "Childe Roland to the Dark Tower Came." It is the peace of "My Life had stood–a Loaded Gun–."

*   *   *

Robert Browning said he wrote "Childe Roland" in one day. He said it came to him in a sort of dream and he simply wrote it down. The careful use of several outside literary sources makes the drama of this statement suspect, but the poem certainly is dreamlike. Living with his wife and small son in Paris, Browning had just finished a long essay on Shelley for a new edition of the poet's *Letters*, when on December 2nd 1851 Louis Napoleon seized power in a coup d'état. On December 4th, the last of the Republican opposition was mowed down in violent street fighting. This was the first time Robert and Elizabeth, witnesses of the violence, disagreed politically. Elizabeth Barrett Browning, an outspoken champion of political liberty, and women's rights, thought that Louis Napoleon would change Europe for the better.

> EMPEROR, Emperor!
> From the centre to the shore,
> From the Seine back to the Rhine,
> Stood eight millions up and swore
> By their manhood's right divine
> So to elect and legislate,
> This man should renew the line
> Broken in a strain of fate
> And leagued kings at Waterloo,
> When the people's hands let go.
> Emperor
> Evermore.
> (EB Browning, "Napoleon III. In Italy," v. 1)

Her husband considered Louis Napoleon just another petty tyrant and distrusted the violent tactics he had used to grasp power. Nearly a month after the coup d'état Browning wrote "Childe Roland." At the time, although he was at work on one of his finest collections of poems, his writing had been ridiculed by English critics and ignored by the reading public. "Sordello" had made him a laughing-stock. Compared to his wife, whose money supported him, whose work he always said he preferred to his own, and whose literary reputation was enormous—compared with the achievement of his favorite poet, Shelley, who had drowned at only thirty, thirty years earlier, the forty-year-old Browning must have been bitter about his own poetic past and future.

> For, what with my whole world-wide wandering,
> What with my search drawn out thro'years, my hope
> Dwindled into a ghost not fit to cope
> With that obstreperous joy success would bring,–
> I hardly tried now to rebuke the spring
> My heart made, finding failure in its scope.
> ("Childe Roland," v. 4)

*   *   *

When Emily Dickinson wrote "My Life had stood–A Loaded Gun–," about eleven years later, she was in her early thirties, unmarried, virtually house-bound by what was probably a severe case of agoraphobia, living with her parents and one unmarried sister in the college town of Amherst. She had been writing hundreds of poems at white heat, in total obscurity. The Civil War was in progress. She had recently made her first move toward an outside reading public by sending a letter, including some of her poems, to the writer and abolitionist Thomas Wentworth Higginson. She must have been wrestling with the knowledge of her extraordinary ability, and the contradiction between visionary illumination–Grace, and simple human longing for worldly recognition.

> I took my Power in my Hand
> And went against the World–
> 'Twas not so much as David–had–
> But I–was twice as bold–
>
> I aimed my Pebble–but Myself
> Was all the one that fell–
> Was it Goliah–was too large–
> Or was myself–too small?

(540)

8. was myself] just myself–/only me–/I–

*   *   *

Before he was executed for leading the attack on Harper's Ferry, John Brown handed a last note to one of his jailors:

Charlestown, Va., Dec. 2, 1859

I, John Brown, am now quite *certain* that the crimes of this *guilty land* will never be purged away but with *blood*. I had, as I now think vainly, flattered myself that without very much bloodshed it might be done.

(*The Life and Letters of John Brown*, p. 620)

At eleven that morning Brown was escorted from prison and put into the wagon that was to carry him to the scaffold. A crowd gathered in the sunlight to watch a human killing. He saw two thousand soldiers, cavalry, and cannon. He looked beyond the crowd to the distant Blue Ridge Mountains. "This is a beautiful country," he said, "I have not cast my eyes over it before, that is, in this direction.''

"My life had stood–a Loaded Gun–" was written during the Civil War. Emily Dickinson, who is so often accused of avoiding political issues in her work, certainly did not avoid them here. As she well knew, the original American conflict between idealism and extremism was being acted out again. John Brown was another puritan zealot invoking Jehovah, set out to fight the Lord's battle, the *Bible*'s way. Liberators and the righteous were, as always, burning, looting and destroying. "Look not to legislatures and churches for your guidance, nor to any soulless *incorporated* bodies, but to *inspirited* or inspired ones," Thoreau had written in "The Last Days of John Brown." *This* Civil War broke something loose in her own divided nature. Now, like Edwards, her intellectual forebear, Dickinson explored the links between service and servitude, without the locks of custom.

*   *   *

ARCHITECTURE OF MEANING

My first thought was, he lied in every word,
   That hoary cripple, with malicious eye
   Askance to watch the working of his lie
On mine, and mouth scarce able to afford
Suppression of the glee that pursed and scored
   Its edge at one more victim gained thereby.
                   ("Childe Roland," v. 1)

I.

My Life had stood—a Loaded Gun
In Corners—till a Day
The Owner passed—identified—
And carried Me away—

My and me. In this unsettling New England lexical landscape
nothing is sure. In a shorter space (woman's quick voice) Dickinson
went further than Browning, coding and erasing—deciphering the idea
of herself, dissimulation in revelation. Really alone at a real frontier,
dwelling in Possibility was what she had brilliantly learned to do.

POSSIBILITIES:

My Life: A Soul finding God.

My Life: A Soul finding herself.

My Life: A poet's admiring heart born into voice by idealizing a precursor poet's song.

My Life: Dickinson herself, waiting in corners of neglect for Higginson
to recognize her ability and help her to join the ranks of
other published American poets.

My Life: The American continent and its westward moving frontier.
Two centuries of pioneer literature and myth had insistently
compared the land to a virgin woman (bride and queen).
Exploration and settlement were pictured in terms of masculine erotic discovery and domination of alluring/threatening
feminine territory.

My Life: The savage source of American myth.

My Life: The United States in the grip of violence that threatened
to break apart its original Union.

My Life: A white woman taken captive by Indians.

My Life: A slave.

My Life: An unmarried woman (Emily Brontë's Catherine Earnshaw) wating to be chosen (identified) by her Lover-husband-Owner (Edgar Linton).

My Life: A frontiersman's gun.

*   *   *

The emblematical Gun escapes its emblem from word one. When MY is identified and carried away, MY becomes anonymous and refuses to budge. Progress seems to be forward but where forward is–uncertain. The first two lines suggest suspended motion, the second two, moving suspension. These first four lines join two souls as they split asunder. Say one thing and mean another. Strange absence of this presence MY is following, or Absence carrying. The only constant is motion and identification of nothing. Symbol is concealment and revelation.

> We do not think enough of the Dead as exhilirants–they are not dissuaders but Lures–Keepers of that great Romance still to us foreclosed–while coveting (we envy) their wisdom we lament their silence. Grace is still a secret.

(Prose fragment 50)

God is hidden. Random subtraction of Love across infinite Empty. Ferocious contradiction. The nuptial Yes, communion confiding, connecting–union with another soul is only another illusion. Humanity must obey mechanical and supernatural necessity. Obedience is necessary for survival, obedience and docility like the lily who toils not. Eve, Lucifer, Edmund, Heathcliff, and Pleasure are reckless and disobedient. I must be obedient to the dominant social system until Death blows the door open. Liberation from life is Death. Will that annihilation be an Orphic transformation or another prison? Was Psyche's lover Eros, or a monster? Emily Brontë and Emily Dickinson, educated, reclusive, visionary women, rebels from a sin-obsessed Fundamentalist religion, *felt* God and Nature separating from each other.

> Each Life Converges to some Centre–
> Expressed–or still–
> Exists in every Human Nature
> A Goal–

Embodied scarcely to itself–it may be–
Too fair
For Credibility's presumption
To mar–

Adored with caution–as a Brittle Heaven–
To reach
Were hopeless, as the Rainbow's Raiment
To touch–

Yet persevered toward–surer–for the Distance–
How high–
Unto the Saints' slow diligence–
The Sky–

Ungained–it may be–by a Life's low Venture–
But then–
Eternity enable the endeavoring
Again.
                                        (680)

   5. Embodied] Admitted
   7. presumption/To mar] temerity to dare–
   9. Adored] Beheld
 11. the] a
 13. surer] stricter–
 15. diligence] industry
 17. by] in–

*   *   *

Wrenched from the Heights, turned aside into an ominous tract, carried from Corners; *unsafe*–the exiles of *Wuthering Heights*, "Childe
Roland To The Dark Tower Came," and "My Life had stood–a Loaded
Gun–" all exist in a phantom and desolate world where life is a void
labor, and Death, Desire's dream. LEAR's world of monstrous necessity
where union with Nature means living outside comfort with the forces
of destruction.

*   *   *

Thomas Wentworth Higginson wrote his ironic "Letter to a
Young Contributor" while waiting to join the Union Army. So far

he had been discouraged in his wish for a regimental appointment. On the day he received Emily Dickinson's first letter in response to his *Atlantic* essay, he had earlier introduced a Miss M.A. Drake to a gathering at the Worcester Gymnasium. Miss Drake was there to put a group of girls through their paces in a wooden dumb-bell exhibition. Higginson was an ardent believer in the beneficial effect of physical exercise for women.

> Do not waste a minute, not a second, in trying to demonstrate to others the merit of your own performance. If your work does not vindicate itself, you cannot vindicate it, but you can labor steadily on something that needs no advocate but itself. . . . Yet do not be made conceited by obscurity, any more than notoriety. Many fine geniuses have been long neglected; but what would become of us if all the neglected were to turn out geniuses? It is unsafe reasoning from either extreme.
>
> ("Letter to A Young Contributor," Sept. 1862)

Higginson was interested enough in Dickinson's letter and enclosed poems to reply immediately by mail, with some show of encouragement and advice. Although during her lifetime he never published even one of her poems, his importance to her was real and abiding. Their correspondence continued for as long as she lived. Higginson carefully saved her letters and the poems she sent him, but his answers to them have been lost. "My Life had stood–a loaded Gun–" in its most literal sense, can be read as her psyche's startled response to her own boldness in hunting him down.

*   *   *

II

> *And now We roam in Sovreign Woods–*
> *And now We hunt the Doe–*
> *And every time I speak for Him–*
> *The Mountains straight reply–*

Conversion is a sort of Death, a falling into Love's powerful attraction. Power is pitiless once you have put it on. The poet is an intermediary hunting form beyond form, truth beyond theme through woods

of words tangled and tremendous. Who owns the woods? Freedom
to roam poetically means freedom to hunt. Is the territory Shakespeare
roamed in sovereign, untouched since and still untouchable? Dickinson antiquely spelt Sovreign as she capitalized the 'S' to both fracture
and fuel its power. Sovereign–European origin.

> The Sovereign is the whole country.
>
> (J. Adams, Def. Constit. Gov. USA)

The United States, peopled by citizens fleeing into freedom, had
no sovereign after the Revolution. Some of these citizens, escaping
religious and political persecution, brought the institution of slavery
along with them.

> Over himself, over his own body and mind,
> the individual is Sovereign.
>
> (J.S. Mill, *Liberty*. 22)

Amerindians found, to their cost, trust in the code word 'sovereign'
could mean all or nothing.

SÓVÉR-EIGN (suv'erin), *a* [Fr. *souverain*; It. *sovrano*; Sp., Port. *soberano*,
from L. *supernus, super*. The early authors, Chaucer, &etc. wrote this
word *soverain, souvereyn*, which were more accordant with the etymology
than the modern spelling.] 1. Supreme in power; possessing supreme
dominion. 2. Supreme; superior to all others; predominant; effectual.
4. Supreme; pertaining to the first magistrate of a nation.

SOV'ER-EIGN (suv'er-in), n. 1. A supreme lord or ruler; one who
possesses the highest authority without control. 2. A supreme magistrate.
3. A gold coin of England, value 20s, or 1 £ sterling.- SYN. King;
prince; monarch; potentate; emperor.
(Noah Webster, *An American Dictionary of the English Language*, 1854)

"God's arbitrary and sovereign good pleasure"

(Jonathan Edwards.)

Dickinson takes sovereignty away from God and bestows it on the
Woods.

*   *   *

> Most sacred vertue she of all the rest,
>   Resembling God in his imperiall might;
>   Whose soueraine powre is herein most exprest,
>   That both to good and bad he dealeth right,
>   And all his workes with Iustice hath bedight.
>   That powre he also doth to Princes lend,
>   And makes them like himselfe in glorious sight,
>   To sit in his owne seate, his cause to end,
> And rule his people right, as he doth recommend.
>   (*Faerie Queene*, V, Proem, v. 10)

The ancient concept of legitimate sovereignty was sacred and sublime. A king, representing God, ruled his subjects by a divinely ordained decree, the allegorical point where God, the State, and human life met. True sanctity surrounded him. Allegiance to this hereditary authority was offered freely by his people, apart from self-interest or arbitrary coercion. Obedience was selfless, idealistic, unquestioning.

> Dread Souerayne Goddesse, that doest highest sit
>   In seate of iudgement, in th'Almighties place,
>   And with magnificke might and wondrous wit
>   Doest to thy people righteous doome aread,
>   That furthest Nations filles with awfull dread.
>   Pardon the boldnesse of thy basest thrall,
>   That dare discourse of so diuine a read,
>   As thy great iustice praysed ouer all:
> The instrument whereof loe here thy *Artegall*.
>   (FQ, V, Proem, v. 11)

During the sixteenth century England was engaged in a battle for survival against the Catholic powers of Europe. Edmund Spenser and many other Elizabethan intellectuals ardently believed in the rightness of Britain's hereditary nobility. Spenser's ceremonial dedications to Elizabeth in the separate books of *The Faerie Queene* extend their shadows and symbols over one another. Illumination of divine influence presiding over human, these paeans to his feminine sovereign, were more than mere flattery, and were essentially unaffected by the real neglect, both literary and political, he suffered at the hands of his thrifty monarch.

Protestant Elizabeth Tudor was enthroned in Edmund Spenser's imagination as Defender of the Faith and emblem of England's power. All pre-connected things of nature moved for him in the holy mystery of her chaste sovereignty. As Gloriana, Una, Belphoebe, Florimell, and Britomart, she rejoins the mystic radiance of the Rose that once was Mary. *Eli sabbath* means Sabbath God in Hebrew. As Britain's sovereign, she was the mediator between man and heaven.

"Elizabeth the Queene of Loue & Prince of Peace"

was also a virgin. Visible symbol of space, finite and feminine, she represented intelligence, chastity, and grace. For Elizabethan poets memory of devotion and willing submission to something ancient, autarchic, and feminine, was still an active element of consciousness, in spite of Protestant historical and religious revision of biblical texts. Elizabeth represented Venus, Diana, Mary, Isolde, Laura, Beatrice–Elizabeth androgynous, even the lost splendor of Isis. In the pre-encyclopaedic sixteenth century, ancient writers, buried cultures, and undreamed of civilizations were being discovered. Language was spoken against an ideal of lost perfection.

Plutarch, who had been initiated into the secret mysteries of Dionysus and believed the soul was imperishable, once translated an epigraph from an Egyptian statue of the Goddess Isis: "I am all that is and all that was and shall be, and no mortal hath lifted my veil." At the blind point between what is said and meant, who is sounding herself? Words open to the names inside them, course through thought in precarious play of double-enchantment, distance. Sovereign secret of initiation . . . Once the mountains were feminine.

> Sweet Mountains–Ye tell Me no lie–
> Never deny Me–Never fly–
> Those same unvarying Eyes
> Turn on Me–when I fail–or feign,
> Or take the Royal names in vain–
> Their far–slow–Violet Gaze–
>
> My Strong Madonnas–Cherish still–
> The Wayward Nun–beneath the Hill–
> Whose service–is to You–

Her latest Worship–When the Day
Fades from the Firmament away–
To lift Her Brows on You–

(722)

*   *   *

Elizabeth had seen that in a world of hereditary authoritarianism, marriage was destructive for a female monarch. After her death, the long European savagery of the Thirty Years War wasn't far off. During the seventeenth century in England and in her North American colonies, the words *sovereign* and *sovereignty* were essential to the intellectual and political battles taking place in philosophical, scientific, and religious debate and rebellion. Old paradigms were being broken, new ones forming. In the wake of profound change came manic religious enthusiasm, and hysteria in the form of persecution that left its mark on nearly everyone, including the early American settlers. For safety, the ''enlightened'' eighteenth century turned God to a sensible watchmaker whose World-clock ticked perfectly. It no longer required winding by him, or by his chosen representatives on earth. After the French Revolution, the antique conception of sovereignty, with all its mixed capacity for evil and for beauty, was effectively broken in the Western world.

*   *   *

To trust in something, be sure, secure. . . . Sovereign lingers on in language, distillation of S, sun–the source, its worldly message muffled, hubris, history, and halting, in the liquid suggestiveness of 'reign'. English pronunciation slides the silent *g* swan-like, across *n* to a vanishing point back of the throat. American–Emily Dickinson cut the treble-syllabled word in two. ''And now We roam in Sovreign Woods–''. Five dissonantal *o*'s in one short line, accent the beauty of the final term.

Full many a glorious morning have I seen
Flatter the mountain-tops with souveraign eye,
Kissing with golden face the meddowes green,
Gilding pale streams with heavenly alchymy;
(Shakespeare, ''Sonnet'' 33)

Janus-faced, *Sovereign*, signifying liberty and submission, is infinitely beguiling.

*   *   *

At the beginning of their separate soliloquies, Browning's Childe Roland and Dickinson's Life find a guide at the limit of the present. Driven by enormous intellectual ambition into the vicinity of the mutilated message of all poetry, they fear the failure of their own energy. Their language must be terse, tense, sometimes violent. England's Elizabethan Laureate lures them with his chivalric questors from earlier fictions. Graceful knights, reclusive hermits, chaste maidens fleeing, doubling, disappearing, or wounding and pursuing. Words hurled through allegorical woods seen backwards through Shakespeare, Bunyan, and Milton.

*   *   *

Gun hovers in subjective space, symbol of her own sway. Gun is only a weapon. Without her Master to grip, aim, and pull her trigger, she has no use. Women of Dickinson's class and century, existed in a legal and financial state of dependence on their fathers, brothers, or husbands, that psychologically mutilated them. Excluded from economic competition (hunting), they were forced to settle for passive consumerism. For a puritan nature, happiness is based on the sacredness of the work ethic. Desire is the process of acquisition. Desire is energy and it is illusory. Time's dominion embraces each poem. Time is Spenser's Blatant Beast, predatory history and unzoned necessity. In the hollow of Merlin's looking glasse, before and after Trojan Aeneas wandered west . . . Sovereignty insists on succession.

Spenser's Blatant Beast is also the Great Beast of Plato. The Great Beast is the social Beast. The crowd or Collective makes wrong seem right because I submit out of false obedience to forced order. The Great Beast may be everything that is remembered by history and all that is most applauded in poetry. What flew away from the crowd and the poet–the meaning she didn't mean, the illusiveness of such allusion alone is truly sovereign.

*   *   *

Meaning has a carnal layering. "My Life had stood–a Loaded Gun–" is concentrated on the lust for power. Two separated souls are leashed together. Day soon turns to night, conversion to cunning, union to sexual aggression. A great poet, carrying the antique imagination of her fathers, requires each reader to leap from a place of certain signification, to a new situation, undiscovered and sovereign. She carries intelligence of the past into future of our thought by reverence and revolt.

To recipient unknown *about 1861*

I am older–tonight, Master–but the love is the same–so are the moon and the crescent. If it had been God's will that I might breathe where you breathed–and find the place–myself–at night–if I (can) never forget that I am not with you–and that sorrow and frost are nearer than I–if I wish with a might I cannot repress–that mine were the Queen's place– the love of the Plantagenet is my only apology–

(L233, from second "Master" Letter)

Q. *Mar.* Plantagenet doth quit Plantagenet,
Edward for Edward pays a dying debt.
(*King Richard III*, IV, iv, 20–21)

*   *   *

CIVIL WOUNDS

Shakespeare's four History Chronicles of the Wars of the Roses are formal fast-paced dramas, arranged in a rigidly patterned ceremonial sequence. During his lifetime they were the most popular of all his plays, but with the exception of *Richard III* they are seldom produced anymore. Each play is an individual structure, inside the wider structure of a group, inside the still wider structure of a political Plan. Their serial form is indebted to the old medieval Mystery plays. Performed in order, like the *Oresteia, Richard III* is the climax. Real history, a Tudor history of retributive Justice, not semi-mythology as in *Lear* and *Macbeth*, dictates the plots. England rests under a curse of civil disorder and blood-

shed for the murder of her Sovereign, Richard II, and as such, the
Lord's anointed.

> Down, down, I come; like glistering Phaeton,
> Wanting the manage of unruly jades.
> In the base court? Base court, where kings grow base,
> To come at traitors' calls, and do them grace.
> In the base court? Come down? Down court! Down king!
> For night-owls shriek, where mounting larks should sing.
> (*Richard II*, III, iii, 178–179)

 So cried Richard before he was captured and murdered. Like Icarus
and Phaeton, Richard Plantagenet, the white rose, mounted too high,
only to plunge down like them, to night and the sea of Death. These
two trace-stories of human sacrifices to the sun haunt Shakespeare's
scenes of ferocious kings and ravening courtiers, as the curse of doom
haunts the land.

*   *   *

> *Clif.*
> Now Phaëton hath tumbled from his car,
> And made an evening at the noontide prick.
> *York.* My ashes, as the phoenix, may bring forth
> A bird that will revenge upon you all:
> (*3 Henry VI*, I, iv, 33–36)

   Triumphant Death is the victor in this nether world of civil
disorder. Protectors are murderers, brothers scorn brothers, marriage
divides and delights to scheme. Basilisks, lizards, serpents, screech-owls,
hedgehogs, toads, tigers, lions, wolves, all beasts of prey and crawling
things match the base and feuding humans. In *3 Henry VI* anarchy rules
the State, each family, and each individual soul. All the main characters
swing helplessly up and down on the Wheel of Fortune–powerless.
The diadem so weakly worn by King Henry, has become a pawn and
paper mockery. Crookback Richard of Gloucester, York's Phoenix,
his most warlike son:

> And yet I know not how to get the crown,
> For many lives stand between me and home;

> And I,–like one lost in a thorny wood,
> That rents the thorns, and is rent with the thorns,
> Seeking a way, and straying from the way;
> Not knowing how to find the open air,
> But toiling desperately to find it out,–
>   (*3 Henry VI*, III, ii, 172–78)

Richard begins to gather into his person the unchecked anarchy around him. Like an actor, writer, artist–like Proteus:

> Why, I can smile, and murther whiles I smile:
> And cry, content, to that which grieves my heart;
> And wet my cheeks with artificial tears,
> And frame my face to all occasions.
> . . . .
> I can add colours to the cameleon;
> Change shapes with Proteus, for advantages,
> And set the murtherous Machiavel to school.
> Can I do this, and cannot get a crown?
> Tut! were it further off I'll pluck it down.
>   (III, ii, 182–5, 191–5)

He assumes his diabolical form. Near the end of *3 Henry VI*, the butcher corners his lamb, Richard comes to kill his King, as Queen Margaret and Clifford had murdered York, his father. The Wheel has come full circle. In the tower of London, Henry VI, gentle grandson of Richard Plantagenet's usurper, proud Bolingbroke, cries out to his own executioner:

> I, Daedalus; my poor boy, Icarus;
> Thy father, Minos, that denied our course;
> The sun, that sear'd the wings of my sweet boy,
> Thy brother Edward, and thyself, the sea,
> Whose envious gulf did swallow up his life.
> Ah, kill me with thy weapon, not with words!
>   (V, vi, 20–28)

Emblem of purity slain, the sun has tumbled down in blaze of blood-red even at noon. The word *sovereign*, repeats obsessively again and again, in bitter mock irony throughout each of these four linked tragedies.

*   *   *

In the Tower's impenetrable secrecy waits melancholy and contagious venom. Here, "false fleeting perjur'd Clarence," will be stabbed, then drowned in a butt of malmsey. Here, Richard, their uncle Protector, will have his two young nephews smothered. Inside this place of covert political action, cold premeditation vies with vengeful justice.

> 1 *Murd*. What we will do we do upon command.
> 2 *Murd*. And he that hath commanded is our king.
> *Clar*. Erroneous vassal! the great King of kings
> Hath in the table of his law commanded,
> That thou shalt do no murther: Will you then
> Spurn at his edict, and fulful a man's?
> Take heed; for he holds vengeance in his hand
> To hurl upon their heads that break his law.
>   (*Richard III*, I, iv, 198–205)

Prophetic Clarence. In this Calvinist universe of Divine Vengeance, his brother Richard represents pure evil, evil without rational explanation. As the Vice, Richard is a necessary villain, the Arch-enemy, a "bottled spider" whose function on earth is to scourge God's errant people for him. Once the Deity's anger is appeased, a new grace will be restored to the suffering nation, and the divided houses of York and Lancaster may unite peacefully in the Tudor marriage of Richmond and Elizabeth.

*   *   *

A tyrant seduces or annihilates. Sorcerer-tyrant Richard seduces by punning. During the progress of *3 Henry VI*, he entered his own capacity for audacious intellectual supremacy. Shakespeare's verbal trickery leaves Richard's fellow characters uncertain about his real meaning, as if uncertainty of *hearing* will prevent these fictive-historical spectres from *seeing*. We, the audience, double in ourselves and applaud as we condemn Richard's mousetrap equivocation. This creature of shadow, whose words cover like a richly embroidered cloak his physical and moral deformities; this chameleon whose genesis was in the violent machinations of a turbulent tetralogy, bursts like gunshot, *solus* into the center of his own Tragedy:

> Now is the winter of our discontent
> Made glorious summer by this sun of York;
> And all the clouds that low'r'd upon our house
> In the deep bosom of the ocean buried.
>   (I, i, 1–4)

Fate has pitched Richard at the impersonal force of History. In his first soliloquy, he undoes the order of things, to reverse and reveal the suspect structure of meaning. His personal and political destiny are in the hands of supernatural and metaphysical Fury before which the individual is a cipher. In this world of inverted moral order, winter is summer, love envy, peace dangerous; and York's son Edward, the King, is idle and lascivious. Richard is honest about one thing—his own ambition. Promises, faith, humanity, filial devotion rate as nothing next to the word 'reward.' The crown, worn by a ruler as symbol of, and reward for power, *is* Elysium. For symbolic power, he will joyfully throw himself against the laws of the world he has violated.

The only character in the Tetralogy who comes close to equalling Richard's equivocal brilliance is Queen Margaret. Like Richard, she is oddly separate from the other characters, like him she is overweeningly ambitious. At the end of *3 Henry VI* she was ransomed back to France, a fugitive, her power utterly lost. She re-appears in *Richard III* as Retribution's mouthpiece, Ate, the Mother-Queen, a ritual figure, soothsayer whose repetitive and appalling curses call down Old Testament vengeance on all who have ever opposed her. Margaret, one of Shakespeare's great women, anticipates Cleopatra and Lady Macbeth. The only character who appears in all four Histories, War's relentless carnage has erased her early beauty and dynamism. Swimming in the aimlessness of violence she had relished, until the death of her lover Suffolk, and her son, Margaret is a harbinger of doom.

Women led by the Mother-Queen are the frame for all four dramas of feuding men. Women, with the exception of Margaret, endure war in paralysis. Throughout the Tetralogy, and especially in *Richard III*, they lend choric structure to the pattern of scheming and murder. In the penultimate scene of Act IV, they gather together, so many Helens and Hecubas, to grieve over their lost sons, husbands, brothers, fathers, friends, and lovers. Into this rhymed antiphonal lamentation, a carefully constructed Ceremonial of women speaking to women, breaks ''hell's black intelligencer,'' Richard:

> A flourish, trumpets!–strike alarum, drums!
> Let not the Heavens hear these tell-tale women
> Rail on the Lord's annointed: Strike, I say.
> (IV, iv, 149–151)

Trumpet and drums reply, inversion of chivalric Roland's horn, like the general trump of doom. War's brass alarum drowns their incantation.

*   *   *

Inside the highly formalized rhetoric of Poetry's reason, stalks unreason of perverted sexuality. Richard's sadistic need to dominate women, the hunter's predatory barbarism, is muffled but not completely muted by Shakespeare's rhymed pattern of wit and wordplay. Wooing and trapping, marriage and murder are linked time and again. The crude savagery of corrupted sovereignty has produced a system of political disequilibrium built on exploitation and coercion.

> *K. Rich.* Say, I will love her everlastingly.
> *Q. Eliz.* But how long shall that title, ever, last?
> *K. Rich.* Sweetly in force unto her fair life's end.
> *Q. Eliz.* But how long fairly shall her sweet life last?
> *K. Rich.* As long as Heaven, and nature, lengthens it.
> *Q. Eliz.* As long as hell, and Richard, likes of it.
> *K. Rich.* Say, I, her sovereign, am her subject low.
> *Q. Eliz.* But she, your subject, loathes such sov'reignty.
> *K. Rich.* Be eloquent in my behalf to her.
> *Q. Eliz.* An honest tale speeds best, being plainly told.
> *K. Rich.* Then, plainly to her tell my loving tale.
> *Q. Eliz.* Plain, and not honest, is too harsh a style.
> *K. Rich.* Your reasons are too shallow and too quick.

> *Q. Eliz.* O, no, my reasons are too deep and dead:—
> Too deep and dead, poor infants, in their graves.
> *K. Rich.* Harp not on that string, madam; that is past.
> *Q. Eliz.* Harp on it still shall I, till heartstrings break.
> (IV, iv, 349–365)

*   *   *

"My Life had stood—a Loaded Gun—" is one of Dickinson's most powerful and puzzling poems. The first verse seems to be a direct response to the first verse of "Childe Roland." In the second, she sizes up Browning's indebtedness to Shakespeare's early history plays for his own Dramatic Monologues. "We want the same things, Shakespeare and myself/ And what I want, I have."/ Bishop Blougram baldly states in his "Apology." That poem, "Instans Tyrannus," "The Last Ride Together," were all included in *Men and Women*. Shakespeare's Richard Gloucester's mode of self-description—he is both villain and Presenter alienated from the characters around him—was repeatedly used by Browning in his own poetry. Childe Roland certainly mimics Richard's participation in Desire's rule breaking especially his self-analysis in *3 Henry VI*.

> Why, then I do but dream on sovereignty;
> like one that stands upon a promontory,
> And spies a far-off shore where he would tread,
> Wishing his foot were equal with his eye;
> And chides the sea that sunders him from thence,
> Saying, he'll lade it dry to have his way:
> (*3 Henry VI*, II, ii, 134–139)

> What in the midst lay but the Tower itself?
>   The round squat turret, blind as the fool's heart,
>   Built of brown stone, without a counterpart
> In the whole world. The tempest's mocking elf
> Points to the shipman thus the unseen shelf
>   He strikes on, only when the timbers start.
> ("Childe Roland," v. 31)

*   *   *

Tudor history with its stern conception of Predestination that downs all individual striving in the inexorable working out of God's Plan for England, punished Richard for the sin of ambition. These Chronicles are the early work of Shakespeare and separate him from the later Tragedies. They were crucial for his development. In them he learned to blend the epic and tragic drama to unite them with history and make something quite new. *Lear* and *Macbeth* are stronger for the knowledge he put on here. Knowledge about the subtle workings of the Body Politic on every citizen, and understanding of what qualities were necessary to make a virtuous leader. A very different faith produced the sovereign humanity of *King Lear*. There tragedy melts into Love's transfiguration. These two poems by Browning and Dickinson are at that place where ambition still includes the idea of domination. Ambition in the nineteenth century was ambiguous at best. Science had replaced Predestination. Technology was slowly but surely snuffing out individuality of production in the name of Progress. "The unseen shelf" an ambitious poet might strike on, was freedom's enslavement to utility. "My Life had stood – a Loaded Gun – " explores the ambiguous terrain of dream, between power and execution, sensuality and sadism – here the poet would tread and draw blood. Trigger-happy with false meaning her poem is an ambiguity of progress, a descant on dissembling. In the second half of this second stanza, she will shrink from being released into the sovereignty of Desire, a force-field as explicit as Death and beyond her will to control.

*   *   *

1865]   *To Louise Norcross*   *March*

I have more to say to you all than March has to the maples, but then I cannot write in bed. I read a few words since I came home – John Talbot's parting with his son, and Margaret's with Suffolk. I read them in the garret, and the rafters wept.

(L304)

Written to her cousin shortly after returning from Cambridge where she had been treated for some mysterious eye trouble, Emily Dickinson who had to carefully conserve her reading, chose passages from 2 and 3 *Henry VI*.

> Q. *Mar.* Enough, sweet Suffolk; thou torment'st thyself;
> And these dread curses, like the sun 'gainst glass,
> Or like an overcharged gun, recoil,
> And turn the force of them upon thyself.
> *Suf.* You bade me ban, and will you bid me leave?
> Now, by the ground that I am banish'd from,
> Well could I curse away a winter's night,
> Though standing naked on a mountain top,
> Where biting cold would never let grass grow,
> And think it but a minute spent in sport.
> (*2 Henry VI*, III, ii, 329–338)

As a great poet, Dickinson possessed the chameleon-capacity to change color in mid-stanza by the manipulation of a word, even one letter. For her own reasons Shakespeare's Tetralogy particularly interested her. It might have simply been the musical word 'Plantagenet.' Probably she instinctively understood the profound linguistic skepticism that forced Shakespeare to undercut what characters in history were saying at the same time they said it. Between 1861 when she probably wrote what was probably her second "Letter to recipient unknown," 1863 when Johnson dates "My Life had stood–a Loaded Gun–", and 1865 when she wrote this letter to Louise Norcross, Emily Dickinson had written many of her finest poems. The American War had been won by the Union Army. The passages she read that March from Shakespeare's History Chronicles concerned another Civil War fought in another country centuries earlier. That war seems to have fictively enveloped her own. All war is the same. Culture representing form and order will always demand sacrifice and subjugation of one group by another.

*　　　　*　　　　*

1865]   A month after she wrote to Louise Norcross, on the evening of April 15th, John Wilkes Booth assassinated Abraham Lincoln while the president was watching a play at Ford's Theatre. Booth came from a famous theatrical family. His father, Junius, and his brother, Edwin, were particularly admired for their performances of *King Richard III*. Edwin's eccentricity and his famous fencing ability often forced the actor playing Richmond to fight for his life on stage.

*   *   *

Edith Sitwell called *Richard III*, Ritual of the Falling of the Sun, and the *Henraid*, a great ritual of Darkness. Eagles and the sun are masculine symbols. An eagle is America's emblem.

> The result showed how well he had calculated, the eagle not even varying his flight, sailing round and round in his airy circle, and looking down, as if in contempt, at his foes.
>
> "Now, Judith," cried Deerslayer, laughing, with glistening and delighted eyes, "we'll see if Killdeer isn't Killeagle, too! . . . A careful sight followed, and was repeated again and again, the bird continuing to rise higher and higher. Then followed the flash and the report. The swift messenger sped upward, and, at the next instant, the bird turned on its side, and came swooping down, now struggling with one wing and then with the other, sometimes whirling in a circuit, next fanning desperately as if conscious of its injury, until, having described several complete circles around the spot, it fell heavily into the end of the ark. . . . "We've done an unthoughtful thing, Sarpent – yes, Judith, we've done an unthoughtful thing in taking life with an object no better than vanity!" exclaimed Deerslayer, when the Delaware held up the enormous bird, by its wings, and exhibited the dying eyes riveted on its enemies with the gaze that the helpless ever fasten on their destroyers.
>
> (JF Cooper, *The Deerslayer*, vol. II, ch. 10)

Killdeer is a hunter's gun. Together We will hunt and kill for pleasure. American frontiersmen were generally men on the make. Land in the West was a commodity to be exploited for profit just as land in the East had been. The Civil War will or will not expiate Our Sin. During the first two Removes of Emily Killdoe's Captivity Narrative of Discovery; the unmentioned sun, blazing its mythopoeic kinship with Sovreign and shooting its rhyme, – flash of sympathy with Gun, has been steadily declining. Dickinson, an unwed American citizen with "–son" set forever in her name, sees God coolly from the dark side of noon.

*   *   *

ATTRACTION INITIATION AND MURDEROUS INTENTION

A brief sketch of a night *fire* hunt.

Two persons are indispensible to it. The horseman that precedes, bears on his shoulder what is called a *fire pan*, full of blazing pine knots, which casts a bright and flickering glare far through the forest. The second follows at some distance, with his rifle prepared for action. No spectacle is more impressive than this pair of hunters, thus kindling the forest into a glare. The deer reposing quietly in his thicket, is awakened by the approaching cavalcade, and instead of flying from the portentous brilliance, remains stupidly gazing on it, as if charmed to the spot. The animal is betrayed to its doom by the gleaming of its fixed and innocent eyes. This cruel mode of securing a fatal shot, is called in hunter's phrase, *shining the eyes.*

The two young men reached a corner of the farmer's field at an early hour of the evening. Young Boone gave the customary signal to his mounted companion preceding him, to stop, an indication that he had *shined the eyes* of a deer. Boone dismounted, and fastened his horse to a tree. Ascertaining that his rifle was in order, he advanced cautiously behind a covert of bushes, to reach the right distance for a shot. The deer is remarkable for the beauty of its eyes when thus *shined*. The mild brilliance of the two orbs was distinctly visible. Whether warned by a presentiment, or arrested by a palpitation, and strange feelings within, at noting a new expression in the blue and dewy lights that gleamed to his heart, we say not, But the unerring rifle fell, and a rustling told him the game had fled. Something whispered him it was not a *deer*; and yet the fleet step, as the game bounded away, might easily be mistaken for that of the light-footed animal.

Daniel Boone had mistaken the species of game. The deer was the sixteen year old daughter of a neighboring farmer fleeing from what she thought was a panther.

The ruddy, flaxen-haired girl stood full in view of her terrible pursuer, leaning upon his rifle, and surveying her with the most eager admiration. "Rebecca, this is young Boone, son of our neighbor," was their laconic introduction. . . . The circumstances of the introduction were favorable to the result, and the young hunter felt that the eyes of the *deer* had *shined* his bosom as fatally as his rifle shot had ever the innocent deer of the thickets. She, too, when she saw the high, open, bold forehead; . . . –the firm front, and the visible impress of decision and fearlessness of the hunter–when she interpreted a look, which said as distinctly as looks could say it, "how terrible it would have been to have fired!" can hardly be supposed to have regarded him with indifference. . . . As for Boone, he was incurably wounded by her, whose eyes he had *shined*, and as he was remarkable for the backwoods attribute of *never being beaten out of his track*, he ceased not to woo, until he gained the heart of Rebecca Bryan. In word, he courted her successfully, and they were married.

> (Timothy Flint, *The First White Man of the West,*
> *or the Life and Exploits of Col. Dan'l Boone*, ch. 1)

Missionary, scientist, geographer, editor, novelist, and poet, Timothy Flint (1780–1840) was the most popular interpreter of the West to the East during the first half of the nineteenth century. His first *Biographical Memoir of Daniel Boone* published in 1833, was a longer version of John Filson's earlier treatment in *Kentucke*, 1784. Flint who had once met Boone, searched carefully through old newspaper articles, interviewed surviving family members, and gathered all the items from local gossip and legend that he could find. From all these elements he formed the most accurate and complete life of Kentucky's pioneer-hunter that was so far available to readers. Although Flint's version of Boone's character was based on fact, those facts artfully arranged produced a gentleman-philosopher. By consciously introducing archetypical imagery into a true story, and frequently comparing the hunter's quasi-mystical "calling" to that of a painter or poet, he rendered the often bloodthirsty rapaciousness of western frontiersmen palatable to an eastern audience.

*　　　　*　　　　*

In 1767 a backwoodsman named Finley, advanced with a few companions, by way of Tennessee, deep into unexplored territory. They came to a gathering of mountains and called them "Enchanted." There, high up on inaccessible cliffs, they saw paintings of the sun, moon, animals and serpents; delineations of another age and race, drawn in colors so brilliant they seemed fresh. The adventurers continued on through a terrestrial paradise teeming with game. In flowering forests and tangled cane-breaks they found deer, elk, buffalo, panthers, foxes – and in open places, pheasants, partridges and turkeys. Timothy Flint tells us that later when Finley and Boone met each other – Boone, while listening to his precursor-hunter describing his travels, felt a sensation "like that of the celebrated painter Correggio, when low-born, untaught, poor, and destitute of advantage, save that of natural endowment, he stood before the work of the immortal Raphael, and said, "I too am a painter!"

> –I wish I were great, like Mr. Michael Angelo, and I could paint for you. You ask what my flowers said – then they were disobedient – I gave them messages. They said what the lips in the West, say, when the sun goes down, and so says the Dawn.
>
> (L187, from second "Master" letter)

"Sister went down to the river and a *painter* [panther] chased her, and she is almost scared to death," exclaimed the Girldeer's uncomprehending brother. The Poem is a fire-hunt, the Poet an animal charmed in one spot, eyes fixed to the light. My precursor attracts me to my future. Fixed purpose is the free spirit of fire. Conversion of consciousness – metamorphosis, may be a flight into wordlessness. Creation was never possession. Daniel Boone willingly cut himself away from civilization's positive progress, in order to re-enter a clear morning of Nature's primeval measuring. To risk the game he married the game and was one with the Wild he would roam. Out of America's text-free past, sounds spelled *kain-tuck-kee* are an Indian place. Boone once said that all a man needed for happiness was "a good gun, a good horse, and a good wife." Lucretia Gunn Dickinson had a tart disposition. Her grand-daughter Emily liked to exclaim when she lost her own temper, or banged a door; "It's not me – it's my grandmother Gunn!" Connections between unconnected things are the unreal reality of Poetry.

*   *   *

'I was only going to say that heaven did not seem to be my home; and I broke my heart with weeping to come back to earth; and the angels were so angry that they flung me out, into the middle of the heath on the top of Wuthering Heights, where I woke sobbing for

joy. That will do to explain my secret, as well as the other. I've no
more business to marry Edgar Linton than I have to be in heaven; and
if the wicked man in there had not brought Heathcliff so low, I shouldn't
have thought of it. It would degrade me to marry Heathcliff, now;
so he shall never know how I love him; and that, not because he's handsome, Nelly, but because he's more myself than I am. Whatever our
souls are made of, his and mine are the same, and Linton's is as different as a moonbeam from lightning, or frost from fire.'

                                                    (*Wuthering Heights*, ch. 9)

Half buried in a moor of memory, the sleepless ghost-lovers of
Wuthering Heights roam the edges of each line of Dickinson's poem.
Children again, their little ice-cold hands scratch the symbol region
of her double meaning. Spell on her window of words the impossibility
of their idyllic unity before the ruthless sweep of Society's civilizing
process. In childhood if we are lucky, Nature furls us in the confidence
of her huge harmony. Assimilation into civilization's chronology, its
grammatical and arithmetical scrutiny calls for correcting, suspecting,
coveting, corrupting my soul into a devious definition of Duty. I must
pursue and destroy what was most tender in my soul's first nature.
A poem is an invocation, rebellious return to the blessedness of beginning again, wandering free in pure process of forgetting and finding.

                          *   *   *

            And every time I speak for Him –
            The Mountains straight reply –

Edgar Linton married Catherine Earnshaw. He loved and now owned her, but he never understood her. Catherine, having betrayed her
integrity, was forced to discard Heathcliff/Herself with her old home
and name. Convention dictated that she must speak as Mrs. Linton –
for Edgar. If she did, Society (The Mountains) would "straight reply"
with a clap of collaborating custom.

                          *   *   *

If Dickinson, the poet, had taken Higginson's advice about her
writing, if she had written as a Victorian poetess should, the literary

world might have "straight replied"; but in the head or heart where her soul lived – where Heathcliff lived in Catherine – she would have lived a liar. The "Mountains straight reply" would have been too straight – confining. Were the Mountains even listening? The man-made Gun's sharp shot is only a reverberating echo of its Owner's own emptiness.

*　　　　*　　　　*

Freedom to explore is a violation of Sovereignty and Avarice, and may be linked forever to loneliness, exile, and murder. Deerslayer in Cooper's Leather-Stocking Tales is a hunter, an adventurous pathfinder, a hero, and a killer. This verse-Gun-Poet-royal "We", dissects the violence of will underlying all relationships of love, all human caring.

> For looking up, aware I somehow grew,
>   'Spite of the dusk, the plain had given place
>   All round to mountains – with such names to grace
> Mere ugly heights and heaps now stol'n in view.
> How thus they had surprised me, – solve it, you!
>   How to get from them was no plainer case.
>   . . . .
> Burningly it came on me all at once,
>   This was the place! those two hills on the right
>   Crouched like two bulls locked horn in horn in fight –
> While to the left, a tall scalped mountain . . . Dunce,
> Fool, to be dozing at the very nonce,
>   After a life spent training for the sight!
>   ("Childe Roland," vv. 28, 30)

*　　　　*　　　　*

III

And I do smile, such cordial light
Upon the Valley glow –
It is as a Vesuvian face
Had let it's pleasure through –

> All the day
> had been a dreary one at best, and dim
> Was settling to its close, yet shot one grim
> Red leer to see the plain catch its estray.
>   ("Childe Roland," v. 8)

What light smiles in this unsurveyed valley of great memory?
Materialistic light from the man-made Gun's forged yellow barrel merely
mincing Nature's pure Idea of light as power, as fire mimics the sun?
What revelation waiting to be born must be shot violently into leering
flame? Now all aspects of the poet's Self are homeless. Mistress of suspicion, what is there, who? Simpering smile of light layer on layer.
Who or what smiler? The Vesuvian face, a mask, veils fire, chaos, original will, vapor. Will that is searing lava and sulfurous power. In the
sovereign solitude of Nature, I *will* all things to be cordial. A smile
of irony curbs the poem's scorching demand for intellectual purity.

In *King Lear*, Edgar having just disguised himself as a mad beg-
gar, sees his blinded father Gloucester:

> My father, poorly led? – World, world, O world!
> But that thy strange mutations make us hate thee,
> Life would not yield to age.
>   (*King Lear*, IV, i, 10–12)

Still Gloucester's disguised outcast son, sane/mad Edgar/Tom, hides
his true identity with a self-righteous capacity for cruelty, strange in
a legitimate hero. Blind outcast Gloucester speaks to air:

> *Old Man.*   You cannot see your way.
> *Glo.* I have no way, and therefore want no eyes;
> I stumbled when I saw: Full oft 'tis seen
> Our means secure us; and our mere defects
> Prove our commodities. – O, dear son Edgar
> The food of thy abused father's wrath!
> Might I but live to see thee in my touch,
> I'd say, I had eyes again!
>   (IV, i, 18–24)

For Edgar and everyone else on this dislocating heath:

Humanity must perforce prey on itself,
Like monsters of the deep.
                              (IV, ii, 49–50)

Love is a fearful power, dragging in its wake the threat of abandon-
ment. Lear's kingdom of exiled Love, is the mythic realm Gun and
Owner have been roaming together.

*   *   *

Who *is* she *that* looketh forth
as the morning, fair as the moon,
clear as the sun, *and* terrible as *an*
army with banners?
                         (*Solomon's Song*, 6:10)

SHE is Desire's dream. In myth at any time, a woman may suddenly change form. Ariadne became a spider, Alcyone, a bird, Niobe,
a stone. Once the North American continent was immeasurable, fer-
tile, pagan–virgin. The European pioneer's predatory nature caused him
to desire and defile her. Fire-myth of the renegade west, a spartan hunter
is its isolate metaphor. James Fenimore Cooper modeled Leather-stocking
on Daniel Boone and other American sons-of-nature figures. In *The
Deerslayer: Or the First War-Path*, Judith Hutter, named for her exotic
and murderous biblical predecessor, gives Nathaniel "Natty" Bumppo,
alias Straight-Tongue, The Pigeon, Lap-ear, Hawk-eye, Deerslayer,
Scout, La Longue Carabine, Pathfinder, Leather-Stocking, her dead false
father's rifle.

"But this is a lordly piece, and would make a steady hand and quick
eye, the King of the Woods!"
"Then keep it, Deerslayer, and become King of the Woods," said
Judith.
                                    (*Deerslayer*, II, ch. 8)

"The talent of composition is very dangerous,–the striking out
the heart of life at a blow, as the Indian takes off a scalp," wrote
Thoreau, borrowing imagery from Cotton Mather's earlier account of
Hannah Dustin's captivity and deliverance. "And what is genius but

finer love?'' asked Emerson. The talent of poetry is splinters of sound, thrown at night and the sun to bring an invisible eagle Emblem in. The poet ''I'' who speaks for ''He'' is nameless ageless dark and light and hidden Vesuvius. Evening in the Valley of Time–My Master is Originator–killer and King.

> I've got a cough as big as a thimble–but I dont care for that–I've got a Tomahawk in my side but that dont hurt me much. [If you] Her master stabs her more–
>
> (L248, from third ''Master'' letter)

In Europe's vanished age of chivalry, a hero's sword was strength wedded to beauty. As long as written memory serves, swords have mystic names and are charmed. Beowulf took Naegling, Sigmund owned Gram, Roland–Durandel, Hauteclère belonged to Oliver; and the Lady of the Lake lent Excalibur to Arthur.

Cooper's knight-errant Narry Bumppo, ''one who might claim descent from European parentage,'' and his Mohican Indian companion, Chingachgook, alias Le Serpent; both keen and restless scout-hunters, move through the peculiar ambiguity of North America's geographically separate and racially blended mythology.

His (Chingachgook's) body, which was nearly naked, presented a terrific emblem of death, drawn in intermingled colors of white and black. His closely shaved head, on which no other hair than the well-known and chivalrous scalping tuft was preserved, was without ornament of any kind, with the exception of a solitary eagle's plume that crossed his crown and depended over the left shoulder. A tomahawk and scalping knife, of English manufacture, were in his girdle; while a short military rifle, of that sort with which the policy of the whites armed their savage allies, lay carelessly across his bare and sinewy knee.

(*The Last of the Mohicans*, vol. I, ch. 3)

Killdeer–Deerslayer's gun, repeats his owner's mystic Indian name in blunter form of English manufacture. In the haunted beauty of our Utopian and bloody pioneer history, love is nature's unnameable grace, Genius preys on God's providence.

*   *   *

GLIMMERGLASS

> "I'm glad it has no name," resumed Deerslayer, "or, at least no
> pale-face name; for their christenings always foretell waste and destruc-
> tion. No doubt, howsever, the red-skins have their modes of knowing
> it, and the hunters and trappers, too; they are likely to call the place
> by something reasonable and resembling." . . . "Among ourselves,
> we've got to calling the place the 'Glimmerglass,' seeing that its whole
> basin is so often fringed with pines, cast upward from its face; as if
> it would throw back the hills that hang over it."
>
> > *(Deerslayer,* I, ch. 2)

Arthur's Excalibur, the magic sword that Beowulf used when he
slew Grendel and Grendel's mother, and Hawk-eye/Deerslayer's
Killdeer – all come from women who lived on or under water. Dickinson has torn the archetypical pattern. My-Life is a woman and a weapon.
Nameless she gives herself to her Self, *then* she serves her Owner/Master.

> –for there was never yet fair woman but she made mouths in a glass.
> > *(King Lear,* III, ii, 35)

> Vesuvius dont talk–Etna–dont [Thy] one of them–said a syllable
> a thousand years ago, and Pompeii heard it, and hid forever–She couldn't
> look the world in the face, afterward–I suppose–Bashful Pompeii! "Tell
> you of the want"–you know what a leech is, dont you–and [remember
> that] Daisy's arm is small–and you have felt the horizon hav'nt you–
> and did the sea–never come so close as to make you dance?
> > (L233, from second "Master' letter)

*   *   *

*Do you promise to love him, comfort him, honour and keep him in sickness
and in health; and forsaking others, keep thee only unto him, as long as ye
both shall live?*

I smiling wife *do* promise these things. Newly identified, *do I*
smother my childhood and my father's name, as my mother smothered
her own? Is my cordial smile artificial? The light, mock light? Was
Brontë's Catherine Earnshaw-Linton, thorn bending to honeysuckle
or honeysuckle bending to thorn? In *Lear* which was Edgar? Cordelia

refused to be falsely cordial to her father. Whose smile? Is the smile Society's Giant pleasure at its Vesuvian power to force me into Custom's lair, or sunshine to warm my cordial acquiescence? There are cords in cordiality.

*   *   *

'Nor I am sure there is no force in eyes

That can doe hurt.'
       Folio: *As You Like It*, Actus Tertius, Scena Quinta

Sounding 'That can doe hurt'–*doe*, the animal, as against *do*, the abstract scar. These eyeing intimacies of print are all actions, as tho 'a soul feminine saluteth us.'

Says Louis Zukofsky near the end of *Bottom: on Shakespeare*.

If they be two, they are two so
  As stiffe twin compasses are two,
Thy soule the fixt foot, makes no show
To move, but doth, if the other doe.
    (John Donne, "A Valediction:
      forbidding mourning," v. 7)

Acquiescence in hunting herself–archaic Doe in sovereign was her own free action. "*Do* I smile. . . . " makes her Bride's soul, the fixt foot unable to move but if the other do, *feminine*.

*   *   *

IV

And when at Night–Our good Day done–
I guard My Master's Head–
'Tis better than the Eider-Duck's
Deep Pillow–to have shared–

Albrecht Dürer said "For in truth art lies hidden with nature, he who can wrest it from her, has it." A lyric poet hunts after some still unmutilated musical wild of the Mind's world. Unconcealed consciousness out in pure Open must be acutely alert if *he* is feminine. At great cost, *She* has been wrested from *My*. Night of the poem has come, sun gone down, Master asleep, his wits have flown into inaccessible forbidden time of sleep memory dream.

> All but Hawk-eye and the Mohicans lost every idea of consciousness, in uncontrollable drowsiness. But the watchfulness of these vigilant protectors neither tired nor slumbered. Immovable as that rock, of which they each appeared to form a part, they lay, with their eyes roving, without intermission, along the dark margin of trees that bounded the adjacent shores of the narrow stream. Not a sound escaped them; the most subtle examination could not have told they breathed.
>
> (*The Last of the Mohicans*, vol. I, ch. 7)

I live in my mind. Oh body of mine, keep watch over my work.

*   *   *

> When at night I go to sleep
> I ask the Lord my Soul to keep.
> If I should die before I wake
> I ask the Lord my Soul to take.
> (Child's Bedtime Prayer)

Childe Emily has switched roles with the Lord. She is *his* guard. Lucifer was flung down from Heaven for such prodigal presumption.

*   *   *

After a good day's writing with her Master's inspiration, the poet, alone, in her clearing of Becoming, keeps on experimenting, deciphering. Melodious thought, product of her Master's head– Beauty, was what she had been breaking and shaping when he sank with the sun into sleeping. At the limits of consciousness perceiving our nakedness, Gun stays awake guarding the Distance. She knows Originality is the discovery of how to shed identity before the magic mirror of Antiquity's sovereign power. Like Edgar/Tom and Deerslayer/Hawk-eye, she escapes the violence of definition, blood of the hunt— by camouflage and cunning. Anonymous dramatic monologue, figment revealing only its own disguising, we will never capture Dickinson in one interpretation. Her soul's deepest necessity was to flee such forced sterility.

*   *   *

TOUCH SHAKESPEARE FOR ME

To Mabel Loomis Todd   *summer 1885*

Brother and Sister's Friend—

"Sweet Land of Liberty" is a superfluous Carol till it concern ourselves—then it outrealms the Birds.

I saw the American Flag last Night in the shutting West, and I felt for every Exile.

I trust you are homesick. That is the sweetest courtesy we pay an absent friend. The Honey you went so far to seek, I trust too you obtain.

Though was there not an "Humbler" Bee?

"I will sail by thee alone, thou animated Torrid Zone."

Your Hollyhocks endow the House, making Art's inner Summer, never Treason to Nature's. Nature will be just closing her Picnic, when you return to America, but you will ride Home by sunset, which is far better.

I am glad you cherish the Sea. We correspond, though I never met him.

I write in the midst of Sweet-Peas and by the side of Orioles, and could put my Hand on a Butterfly, only he withdraws.

Touch Shakespeare for me.

The Savior's only signature to the Letter he wrote to all mankind, was, A Stranger and ye took me in.

America
(L1004)

The lyric poet reads a past that is a huge imagination of one form. Dante, Chaucer, Spenser, Shakespeare, Donne, Milton, Keats, Shelley, Wordsworth, Tennyson, and Browning, were for her intermediaries of that form. A band of brothers and a European Quest. In her letter to Mabel Todd, the fifty-five year old Emily Dickinson quoted Emerson and signed herself "America." Her history of poetry, with the exception of Sappho, Emily Brontë, and Elizabeth Barrett Browning, was the chronicle of another sex and continent. She, who converted every obstacle to rich material, never stopped writing about Liberty, Exile, Origin.

> Undue Significance a starving man attaches
> To Food—
> Far off—He sighs—and therefore—Hopeless—
> And therefore—Good—
>
> Partaken—it relieves—indeed—
> But proves us
> That Spices fly
> In the Receipt—It was the Distance—
> Was Savory—
>
> (439)

* * *

> Behold yon' simpering dame,
> Whose face between her forks presageth snow;
> That minces virtue, and does shake the head
> To hear of pleasure's name;
> The fitchew, nor the soiled horse, goes to't
> With a more riotous appetite.
> Down from the waist they are centaurs, though women all above: but
> to the girdle do the gods inherit, beneath is all the fiends'; there's hell,
> there's darkness, there is the sulfurous pit, burning, scalding, stench,
> consumption;—Fye, fye, fye! pah; pah! Give me an ounce of civet; good
> apothocary, sweeten my imagination: there's money for thee.
>
> (*King Lear*, IV, vi)

"While Shakespeare remains," wrote Dickinson in a letter to Higginson, "Literature is firm." If her favorite author at the height of his power demonstrated his volcanic loathing for women, constantly colliding with his own aversion, he revealed and reviled it in a play tender beyond comparison. In *King Lear* Shakespeare has gone down to the deeps of sexual terror, into the violence of primal exile from our mother. Homesick and in homeless isolation every soul comes crying here. Locked alone in the vision of my brain, even language never

truly connects me to another. When we are born we 'wawl and cry'.
Love succumbs predestined to obey. All lendings off, meaning utterly
unsafe, I destroy what I love and love is joy.

> Drama's Vitallest Expression is the Common Day
> That arise and set about Us–
> Other Tragedy
>
> Perish in the Recitation–
> This–the best enact
> When the Audience is scattered
> And the Boxes shut–
>
> "Hamlet" to Himself were Hamlet–
> Had not Shakespeare wrote–
> Though the "Romeo" left no Record
> Of his Juliet,
>
> It were infinite enacted
> In the Human Heart–
> Only Theatre recorded
> Owner cannot shut–
>
>   (741)
>
> 5. best enact] more exert
> 10. left] leave
> 12. infinite] tenderer–
> 15. Never yet was shut–

In the Theatre of the Human Heart, necessity of poetic vocation
can turn creator to corruptor, collide fear and force with ideal beauty,
line and verse. Grace must hunt down the soul, recapture the will. On
Lear's heath and Roland's grey plain, language and nature have broken
the order of each other. So have Dickinson's anonymous Gun and
Owner. My has a capital "M" beside Master. Hope dwindled to ar-
rival the heroic ideal may have been a lie and the "round squat turret"
blind as the fool's heart," an elf to mock and point too late. But
mechanical empiricism is also a lie. Connotative definition broods and
breeds nesting. The Eider-Duck leads her own life of allegory.

EÌDER   )
EÌDER-DUCK)ⁿ. [G., Sw. *eider*]

A species of sea-duck found in the Shetland Isles, the Orkneys, &etc., and producing uncommonly fine down.

EiDER-DOWN (īder-), *n.* Down or soft feathers of the eider duck. (Noah Webster, *An American Dictionary of the English Language*, 1854)

The female eider plucks from her breast the down that lines her nest. If the first downy lining and eggs are taken by down gatherers, she makes another lining and lays more eggs. Her mate denudes his breast if a third lining is needed.

In Europe, the down was highly valued, so the birds were sheltered and carefully conserved. Some became as tame as hens, and would allow their owners to stroke them.

In North America, the birds were killed for their feathers, as their flesh was considered worthless. By the late eighteenth century Eiders were so rare that even feather hunting was considered a waste of time and profit. Eider-down was imported from Europe.

Still, hunters and fishermen killed the birds for sport, and for their eggs. By the end of the 1800s the vast Eider nurseries of the Labrador Coast were only a legend. In Dickinson's time, the Eider was rare but not extinct. They occupied the outer ledges of rocks that jutted into the ocean. Massachusetts gunners called them Sea Ducks.

*   *   *

Deep Pillow was a warm bed and safe house if Dickinson took Higginson's advice and altered the eccentricity of her poems to suit the taste of her time. "'Tis better than the Eider-Duck's/Deep(low)Pillow – to have shared – ." The playful but frigidly artificial 'Tis' reins in her revolutionary desire to *join* the wild eider outside in cold weather.

A newly married wife shares her pillow with her husband even if what she rests her head on is the freedom she has plucked from her own breast. Deep was chosen over low. Deep calls to Deep, suggesting death and drowning. Emily Brontë's persona Catherine Linton, driven mad by her inability to detach Heathcliff from herself, and remorse over marrying Edgar, echoed Ophelia. Dickinson's two lines echo Catherine.

Tossing about, she increased her feverish bewilderment to madness, and tore the pillow with her teeth, then raising herself up all burning, desired

that I would open the window. We were in the middle of winter, the
wind blew strong from the north-east, and I objected. . . . A minute
previously she was violent; now, supported on one arm, and not notic-
ing my refusal to obey her, she seemed to find childish diversion in pulling
the feathers from the rents she had just made, and ranging them on
the sheet according to their different species: her mind had strayed to
other associations. 'That's a turkey's,' she murmured to herself; 'and
this is a wild-duck's; and this is a pigeon's. Ah, they put pigeons' feathers
in the pillows—no wonder I couldn't die! Let me take care to throw
it on the floor when I lie down. And here's a moor-cock's; and this–I
should know it among a thousand–it's a lapwing's. Bonny bird; wheeling
over our heads in the middle of the moor. It wanted to get to its nest,
for the clouds touched the swells, and it felt rain coming. This feather
was picked up from the heath, the bird was not shot–we saw its nest
in the winter, full of little skeletons. Heathcliff set a trap over it, and
the old ones dare not come. I made him promise he'd never shoot a
lapwing, after that, and he didn't. Yes, here are more! Did he shoot
my lapwings, Nelly? Are they red, any of them? Let me look.'
      'Give over with that baby-work!' I interrupted, dragging the pillow
away, and turning the holes towards the mattress, for she was remov-
ing its contents by handfuls. 'Lie down and shut your eyes, you're
wandering. There's a mess! The down is flying about like snow!'
                                                    (*Wuthering Heights*, ch. 12)

Deep calls again to Deep suggesting Death and smothering.

                                                             Late summer 1885

      Mattie will hide this little flower in her friend's Hand. Should she
ask who sent it, tell her as Desdemona did when they asked who slew
her, "Nobody–I myself."

                                                                    (L1010)

Emily Dickinson knew that sharing the Duck's Deep Pillow would
have meant slaying her own genius.

                         *   *   *

The Eider-Duck has torn apart all interpretation of place and progress
in Dickinson's poem. Sleepless at night, habit shot all senses alert–

guarded answers are loaded questions. Liberty looks like banishment. Deep Pillow slides in another echo of an echo, Keats' "Bright Star." In the nineteenth century it was simply called "The Last Sonnet." He wrote it on a blank page, in his edition of Shakespeare, facing "A Lover's Complaint," another account of Chastity wavering. It seems to speak of Keats' readiness as he neared death to exchange the loneliness poetic ambition had brought him for Fanny Brawne's love and the warmth of domestic affection. Love for letters wavering, words turn relentlessly from meaning to melting meaning, lyric intensity swooning into the pull of its own gravity.

> BRIGHT star, would I were stedfast as thou art—
>   Not in lone splendour hung aloft the night
> And watching, with eternal lids apart,
>   Like nature's patient, sleepless Eremite,
> The moving waters at their priestlike task
>   Of pure ablution round earth's human shores,
> Or gazing on the new soft-fallen mask
>   Of snow upon the mountains and the moors—
> No—yet still stedfast, still unchangeable,
>   Pillow'd upon my fair love's ripening breast,
> To feel for ever its soft fall and swell,
>   Awake forever in a sweet unrest,
> Still, still to hear her tender-taken breath,
> And so live ever—or else swoon to death.
>   (Keats, "Sonnet")

She the man-made Gun; Poet influenced by the work of many men, tied by a cord of attachment to her Master, may be shut in a prison of admiration that seals her from a deeper region of herself—a mapless dominion, valueless value, sovereign and feminine, outside the realm of dictionary definition, the selflessness of filial benediction swelling forever under human uprootedness in fiction, the love beyond words to tell, some women feel for their children. Human savagery has broken the bond between civilization and the Eider. Feathers from her nest were pain plaiting peace—anonymous spontaneous creation. Love builds her nest for soft shelter. At her baby's cry, milk runs in the breast of each mother. The sacramental source of Genius may be *outside* with

the Eider on her ledge beyond predators. The source of Genius is pillowed
on the breast of Nature. Cold words are powerless to kill into life her
unsayable unchangeable Gentleness.

*   *   *

Thus nine dayes I sat upon my knees, with my Babe in my lap,
all my flesh was raw again; my Child being even ready to depart this
Sorrowfull world, they bade me carry it out to another Wigwam (I
suppose because they would not be troubled with such spectacles)
Whither I went with a very heavy heart, and down I sat with the pic-
ture of death in my lap. About two houres in the night, my Sweet
Babe, like a Lambe departed this life, on Feb.18.1675. It being *six yeares,
and five months* old. It was *nine dayes* from the first wounding, in this
miserable condition, without any refreshing of one nature or another,
except a little cold water. I cannot but take notice, how at another time
I could not bear to be in a room where any dead person was, but now
the case is changed; I must and could ly down by my dead Babe, side
by side all the night after.

(Rowlandson, *Narrative*, "The Third Remove," pp. 10–11)

What redemptive vision can transform the radical chaos of one
wounded child's slow and agonizing death in the ahuman continuous-
ness of a virgin forest? Where is the warm hearth Heidegger finds
through Hölderlin's perception of what lies waiting at the summit of
the central Self? Before World War II could any work of European
imagining exceed the rough-hewn intensity of this American Puritan
mother's prophesy?

During the progress of Dickinson's idiosyncratic paean to Primi-
tivism, the wilderness that is a clear resemblance of the World, has
become increasingly threatening. Now this half-barbarous mistress of
Microcosm scouts alone and alert in her clearing. Beyond the control
of her redemptive imagination hosts of forgotten pioneer women lie
sleeping–*South-west*–where Indian souls go at last. And there are the
children carried captive from home who were never seen again.

From their Sleeping: The Observation generall.
Sweet rest is not confind to soft Beds, for, not only God gives
his beloved sleep on hard lodgings: but also Nature and Custome gives

sound sleep to these Americans on the Earth, on a Boord or Mat. Yet how is *Europe* bound to God for better lodging, &c.

More Particular
1. *God gives them sleep on Ground, on Straw,*
   on Sedgie Mats or Boord:
When English softest Beds of Downe,
   sometimes no sleep affoord.
          (Roger Williams, *A KEY to the LANGUAGE*
                    of AMERICA, p. 21)

         *   *   *

V

To foe of His – I'm deadly foe –
None stir the second time –
On whom I lay a Yellow Eye –
Or an emphatic Thumb –

Death and slavery enter the poem with the voiceless affliction of the Eider. Who is civilized, who savage is an open question, seer and seen unknown. In the domain of "My Life had stood – a Loaded Gun –" systems of meaning meet, only to subvert their original intention, foe and foe forming lines of fire between one another. In a system of Justice, rebellion destroys all order. The three most serious threats to the political and religious stability of the Commonwealth of Massachusetts in the seventeenth century – the Antinomian controversy – 1636, the Quaker persecutions of the 1650s and the Witchcraft hysteria in 1692 – all directly involved women. For the Puritan mind, consciousness of innocence in corners thrown, must be emphatically rubbed down by rigorous dedication to "duty" and monotonous repetition of devotion.

In Civil War, history collapses on itself. Shakespeare's "triumphant Death smear'd with captivity" laughs to show the truth of human frailty. Ties bind us to the past in pain. For the young American Republic, the 1860s were tragic years of human demolition and civil disorder. The terrifying nature of existence had once again come home, vivid reminder that God may indeed hold us over the pit of hell, "much as one holds a spider or some loathesome insect over the fire –."

Jonathan Edwards, Emily Brontë, and Emily Dickinson looked into

the core of eternal destruction. They greeted what they saw with affirmation and elation. Nothing is more imperious than the way ''My Life
had stood–a Loaded Gun–'' leaps from the center of fascicle 34. In
this verse Dickinson puts on the mask of diabolism to speak with the
voice of the Destroyer. Gun exults in her Calvinist rejection of
moderation.

> Pain–expands the Time–
> Ages coil within
> The minute Circumference
> Of a single Brain–
>
> Pain contracts the Time–
> Occupied with Shot
> Gammuts of Eternities
> Are as they were not–
>
>   (967)
>
> 2. coil] lurk
> 7. Gammuts] Triplets
> 8. Are] flit–/ Show–

*   *   *

In Civil War we are all mutually entangled. To be rebellious but
to distrust rebellion comes easily to women who may lose their husbands
and children. To be rebellious and to distrust rebellion is the plight
of the tragic artist. Daring is dangerous. In this poem early pleasure
so falsely cordial quickly grows truly hostile. Shakespeare's devil Richard
III to his future brides; Othello to Desdemona, Goneril and Regan–.
God's sovereignty *is* his personality, authoritarian and legalistic, command and decree. Lear rashly gave his world away. Balance, confu-
sion, naming, transformation–. Arrived at the point of initiation, stopped at the moment of conversion, instinct draws up short.

*   *   *

Loki, Lucifer, Richard, Edmund, Iago, Heathcliff, Magua–
estranged from reliable familiarity, face to face with Poetry–Lies, and
living dangerously. Arrived at my precursor's essential nature, abstracted
and abandoning, Nature has no origin. Chaos and violence of my own

hands clapping. Corrupted by the cruelty in beauty, is Art a luxury or necessity?

On Sitting Down To Read King Lear Once Again:

> O GOLDEN tongued Romance, with serene lute!
>   Fair plumed Syren, Queen of far-away!
>   Leave melodizing on this wintry day,
> Shut up thine olden pages, and be mute:
> Adieu! for, once again, the fierce dispute
>   Betwixt damnation and impassion'd clay
>   Must I burn through; once more humbly assay
> The bitter-sweet of this Shakespearian fruit:
> Chief Poet! and ye clouds of Albion,
>   Begetters of our deep eternal theme!
> When through the old oak Forest I am gone,
>   Let me not wander in a barren dream,
> But, when I am consumed in the fire,
> Give me new Phoenix wings to fly at my desire.
>   (Keats, ''Sonnet'')

Keats said Shakespeare was the sea. King Lear is nature.

*   *   *

''To foe of His–I'm deadly foe–'' Here, at the verge of Meaning's confine, creation and destruction, covert communication, War is the father of us all. Naming near Night's border, the Wife-Pillow-Gun-Poetess writing humbly to Thomas Wentworth Higginson for advice has been irretrievably lost. I do not want pity. I transfer to others the hate in my humiliated heart.

*   *   *

> A paleness took the poet's cheek:
> 'Must I drink *here*?' he seemed to seek
> The lady's will with utterance meek:
>
> 'Ay, ay,' she said, 'it so must be;'
> (And this time she spake cheerfully)
> 'Behoves thee know *World's cruelty*.'
>   (EB Browning, ''A Vision of Poets,'' vv. 60–61)

Elizabeth Barrett Browning, whose tragic sense of the injustices stalking Victorian living was a catalyst for her husband's writing and for Emily Dickinson, failed as a poet herself, because she thought formal linear progression of plot through forward moving time of a poem was enough for its telling. In fact, Faraday's quest for Unity might have been applied to writing poetry:

An entirely new relation of natural forces.

An analysis of gravitational source.

A justification of the conservation of force.

Good intentions prove nothing. Faith proves nothing. Velocity and force of violent motion, gunfire at every human soul in every blind nation struggling. Victorian scientists, philosophers, historians, intellectuals, poets, like most contemporary feminist literary critics–eager to discuss the shattering of all hierarchies of Being–didn't want the form they discussed this in to be shattering. In her own time, Elizabeth Barrett Browning's way of poetically puzzling over human nature, changing reality, political revolution, slavery, sexual exploitation, brutality, and economic necessity, was extremely popular. Ruskin, Swinburne, and even Rilke, who translated her *Sonnets from the Portuguese*, admired her. Swinburne went so far as to compare her to Shakespeare. For the Robert Browning of "Childe Roland," and even more for Emily Dickinson, who was geographically separated from European custom, the past, that sovereign source, must break poetic structure open for future absorption of words and definition. Velocity, mechanics, heat, thermodynamics, light, chaos of formulae, electromagnetic induction must be called back into the Sublime, found and forgotten. Dickinson was expert in standing in corners, expert in secret listening and silent understanding. Bristling with Yankee energy, chained to an increasingly demanding agoraphobia, she moved through that particular mole of nature in her–she studied Terror. Adopted parataxis and rupture to tell the feverish haste, the loss, to warn of storm approaching–Brute force, mechanism. Cassandra was a woman. All power, including the power of Love, all nature, including the nature of Time, is utterly unstable.

Banish Air from Air –
Divide Light if you dare –
They'll meet
While Cubes in a Drop
Or Pellets of Shape
Fit.
Films cannot annul
Odors return whole
Force Flame
And with a Blonde push
Over your impotence
Flits Steam.

(854)

Power is a vital necessity for the powerful. They must protect each other at all cost and against all foes. The Master makes his worker fear him because of his own fear. The family and woman's position in it, slavery, fate of the eider, are the image of a wide world order. Power of the state corrupts us all. Cold War. A Gun is inert matter. Weapons don't fire themselves. Mary Rowlandson's ten year old daughter Mary, was "taken from the door at first by *a Praying Ind* & afterward sold for a gun." "Now Judith," cries Cooper's hero, Deerslayer/Hawkeye, "we'll see if Killdeer isn't Killeagle, too!"

When I love a thing I want it and I try to get it. Abstraction of the particular from the universal is the entrance into evil. Love, a binding force, is both envy and emulation. HE (the Puritan God) is a realm of mystery and will always remain unknowable, authoritarian, unpredictable. Between revealed will and secret will Love has been torn in two.

DUALISM: Pythagoras said that all things were divisible into two genera, good and evil; in the genus of good things he classified all perfect things such as light, males, repose, and so forth, whereas in the genus of evil he classified darkness, females, and so forth.

(Thomas Aquinas, "On the Power of God," p. 84)

Promethean aspiration: To be a woman and a Pythagorean. What *is* the communal vision of poetry if you are curved, odd, indefinite, irregular, feminine. I go in disguise. Soul under stress, thread of connection broken, fusion of love and knowledge broken, visionary energy lost, Dickinson means this to be an ugly verse. First I find myself a Slave, next I understand my slavery, finally I re-discover myself at liberty inside the confines of known necessity. Gun goes on thinking of the violence done to meaning. Gun watches herself watching.

> No Bobolink–reverse His Singing
> When the only Tree
> Ever He minded occupying
> By the Farmer be–
>
> Clove to the Root–
> His Spacious Future–
> Best Horizon–gone–
> Whose Music be His
> Only Anodyne–
> Brave Bobolink–
>   (755) 11 in fascicle 34
> 5. Root] Core
> 7. Best] All
> 7. gone] known–

           *   *   *

GUN, *n.* [W.gwn; Corn. *gun.*] An instrument consisting of a barrel, or tube, of iron or other metal, fixed on a stock, from which balls, shot, or other deadly weapons are discharged by the explosion of gunpowder. The larger species of *guns* are called *cannon*, and the smaller species are called muskets, *carbines*, fowling-pieces, &etc. GUN, *v.* i.To shoot.

(Websters American Dictionary)

    Voiced Sound
      T H U M B

    MY, feminine Gun, waited powerless at home until the *Springfield Republican* newspaper told her that Thomas Wentworth Higginson, her literary life-line, was gone with all other healthy men to fight for the Union Army. Northern women, children, the maimed, infirm, and old men, waited at home until war was done. A Slave was often referred to as a child, a Woman as a girl. An original Disobedience: A girl in bed alone sucking her thumb. *Thumb*: short thick first or most preaxial digit of the human hand differing from the four fingers in having greater freedom of movement and being opposable to the other fingers. *Thumb* and *Gnome* have silent letters and rhyme wrongly with *Gun* and *whom*. For Freudians, thumb and gun are phallic and the same. Without a thumb it would be hard to grip a gun. The thumb helps my fingers grip, helps to turn the pages of a book. *All thumbs*–Awkward. *Under the thumb*: under control of. *Thumb*: To feel point press attack . . . to play. To thumb one's nose at the collective wisdom of the ages. Wives and slaves were thumbs. In the nineteenth century a mark made with the inked thumb was used for identification of an illiterate person. Thumb rhymes with dumb. *Thumb* a nursery word rhymes crookedly with 'time' riddled back to Jack Horner who sat in his corner, eating a Christmas Pie. He put in his thumb pulled out a plum and said "What a good boy am I!" Good Uncle Tom. Was Jack put in the corner because he was wrong or dumb? What had he done? Back around to *foe* and *Master* and Jack the Giant Killer climbing his beanstalk ladder to hear the "*Fie, foh, and fum,*" of Edgar/Tom's mad song, "I smell the blood of a British man./ Be he alive or be he dead,/ I'll grind his bones to make my bread." Jack, and Jacob the *Bible's* poet, were both ladder-watchers. Tom Thumb ("Your Gnome") was little but as powerful as David the other biblical poet, who slew Goliath with a sling-shot. Cover the touch-hole of a cannon with your thumb. She, GUN-THUMB-YELLOW EYE-BULLET-POET-GNOME is emphatic. Dauntless predator and protector.

To T. W. Higginson   *spring 1886*

I have been very ill, Dear friend, since November, bereft of Book and Thought, by the Doctor's reproof, but begin to roam in my Room now–

I think of you with absent Affection, and the Wife and Child I have never seen, Legend and Love in one–

Audacity of Bliss, said Jacob to the Angel "I will not let thee go
except I bless thee"–Pugilist and Poet, Jacob was correct–

Your Scholar–

(1042)

*   *   *

Thomas Wentworth Higginson: 1823–1911

She was much too enigmatical a being for me to solve in an hour's interview, and an instinct told me that the slightest attempt at direct cross-examination would make her withdraw into her shell; I could only sit and watch, as one does in the woods; I must name my bird without a gun, as recommended by Emerson.

(T. W. Higginson recalling his meeting with Emily Dickinson twenty years after the fact in the *Atlantic Monthly*, October 1891)

Thomas Wentworth Higginson, so often pictured as a cautious conservative by Dickinson scholars, was far from that in his youth and middle age. Descended from leaders of New England's Puritan theocracy he was a grandson of Stephen Higginson, one of Salem's great shipping merchants, who had served in the Continental Congress, and the Massachusetts Legislature. Thomas was the youngest in a family of fifteen children. A precocious and privileged child, he passed the examinations for entrance to Harvard University at only thirteen. After graduation, Higginson went on to Divinity School, and eventually became a Unitarian minister in Newburyport, Massachusetts. Like Edwards, Timothy Flint, and Emerson, Higginson's restless intelligence soon brought him into conflict with his parish. A valued friend and advisor of Lucy Stone, Margaret Fuller, and Susan B. Anthony, Higginson was always an outspoken advocate for women's rights. His essay, *Woman and Her Wishes*, one of the first feminist tracts, was widely distributed in America and England. Higginson was also an ardent abolitionist many years before that cause became popular. He was one of a group who tried to rescue Anthony Sims, in one of the earliest fugitive slave incidents. In 1848 he ran unsuccessfully for Congress on the Free State ticket. This was the last straw for the rich shipowners in his Congregation who for their own reasons didn't wish to see slavery questioned, or women voting, and Higginson was dismissed.

After the passage of the Fugitive Slave Act in 1850, Higginson joined the bitter agitation against it. In Worcester, fifty miles west of Boston, a Free Unitarian Church similar to Theodore Parker's had been organized. In 1852, Higginson, who was by then a popular writer and well known public speaker, was asked to become their minister. Worcester was near the main line of the Underground Railroad, and during the increasingly disturbed years before the outbreak of the Civil War, he helped to pass runaway slaves through Boston to a safe farm in the area. In 1854 he was the leader in a bungled attempt to free Anthony Burns from the Boston Courthouse. During the violent struggle that broke out, a guard was killed, and Burns recaptured. This was the most sensational of the fugitive slave incidents and deputy's death was an embarrasment to the Abolitionist Cause. Theodore Parker, Wendell Phillips, and Thomas Higginson were all indicted, but the case never

came to trial. Furious at the cowardice of the Massachusetts judicial
system, Higginson in Worcester preached a sermon ''Massachusetts
in Mourning'' that caused a furor and was widely distributed. Emily
Dickinson, an avid newspaper reader, and resident of a nearby town,
would almost certainly have seen it.

After the passage of the Kansas-Nebraska Bill, Kansas was the center of violent conflict. Organizations from New England were raising
money for relief of the settlers, and Higginson journeyed there to report directly on the conflict for the *New York Tribune*. When James
H. Lane, who called himself ''Major General commanding the Free-
State forces of Kansas'' and was a cohort of John Brown, suddenly
appointed Higginson a ''Brigadeer General'' and a member of his staff,
the Unitarian minister turned war correspondant, found himself cast
in the role of a guerilla soldier. Many years later he remembered that
time in *Poet Lore*:

> There are doubtless many beside myself who possess some book
> that has in it some single written date or memorandom which may al-
> most be said to mark a turning point in the owner's life; some point
> to which all that went before it had led, whether he knew it or not,
> and by which all that followed it was influenced. Around such a record
> a whole group of personal associations will probably cluster, like lookers-
> on, possibly more real and permanent to us than any living witness.
> For myself I have more than one such memorial, but that which has
> stood out among them all for more than forty years is a page where
> two lines of poetry are underscored in pencil and the initials added
> ''L.K.T., Oct. 7, 1856.'' These initials are not those of a man or maid,
> but are the memorial of a halt made one day when I was riding, being
> armed for the first time in my life, through the then debatable ground
> between Kansas and Nebraska, in charge of an armed party of emigrants
> towards the beseiged town of Lawrence. The book is Browning's 'Men
> and Women.' The lines are:
>
>> ''Fool, to be dozing at the very nonce,
>> After a life spent training for the sight!''
>
> and they are taken from the poem ''Childe Roland to the Dark Tower
> Came.''
>
> I have since been in more responsibilities and in greater dangers;
> but this was the moment of which it might be said, as Carlyle's hero says

in 'Sartor Resartus,' "After this I immediately began to become a man." That I should have carried in my pocket to Kansas only that one book, that out of all its pages have marked that one passage, is a fact to me of more value as a testimonial of the 'Childe Roland' poem than any other could be. It shows that I carried it for a sort of elixir of life, and used it for that purpose. What it did for me it must have done for others . . .

The 'Childe Roland' poem is simply Browning's profoundest attempt to touch the mystery of life. The Dark Tower stands for the supreme secret of each man's existence: we follow up streams, tread mountains, and reach only this at last. Friends and foes help to guide us to it; but we must go alone. The last finger extended may even be that of a malicious enemy. We may so shrink from it that the sky looks dark, the whole surroundings repulsive. All our early memories come back upon us, veiled in a shadowy mist; yet we go forward. This is the poem. The critics exhaust their variety of conjecture to show what it all means. Dr. Furnivall states that he asked Browning three times whether the poem was an allegory, and that Browning had said each time that it was simply dramatic–as if any human being could tell where "dramatic" ends and "allegory" begins! Given what is dramatic enough, and every human being may draw its own allegory from it. Mr. Kirkman and Mr. Sears Cook think the tower means death; Mrs. R. Gratz Allen interprets the moral as lying in sin and punishment; Mrs. Orr and Mrs. Drewry find that it stands for life and truth; Professor Arlo Bates "can think of nothing more heroic, more noble, more inspiring," than the whole poem. As I said every man finds in it his own tower; and, the more towers suggested, the greater tribute to the spell woven by Browning. Life's supreme mystery,–that is the Dark Tower.

All his life, Higginson at heart a gentle person, was fascinated by wanderers, outlaws, and rebels. Many of his articles show his desire to understand the motivation behind violent political rebellion. Between 1860 and 1862 he wrote a series of pieces for the *Atlantic Monthly* about slave uprisings during the early part of the century. "The Maroons of Surinam," "The Maroons of Jamaica," "Nat Turner's Insurrection," and the insurrections of "General" Gabriel in 1800, and Denmark Vesey in 1822, are still interesting today. At the time he wrote them, most information about the uprisings could only be obtained from wildly exaggerated accounts in Southern newspapers. Higginson charted his search for some truth through the myriad accounts of panicked whites, and the resulting propaganda in the media, constantly stressing the irony of White truth as opposed to Black.

A close reading of "Nat Turner's Insurrection" shows that "My Life had stood–a Loaded Gun–" may have been triggered by parts of it.

In 1856 his enthusiasm for reckless daring in others drew him to the figure of John Brown. Higginson and Theodore Parker, among other conspirators, saw in Brown's ideas for violent insurrection the last best hope of forcing the United States Government to see that slavery must be abolished. In 1859 Thomas Higginson was one of the Secret Six who plotted with Brown, the result being the tragic raid at Harper's Ferry. After Brown's capture, all the other co-conspirators fled to Europe or Canada, in one case a mental hospital, in order to escape the scandal and possible arrest. Not only did Higginson stay at home, but he stated publicly that he wished he had been with Brown at Harper's Ferry. He visited the Brown family and wrote an article about their heroism, plotted Brown's escape from jail, and when that possibility failed, he organized a group of citizens including Thoreau and Emerson, to raise money for Brown's defense.

After this period of public militancy, influenced by his friend Thoreau, Higginson turned to nature for solace, and wrote a series of articles about flowers and birds for the *Atlantic*. Dickinson read them all carefully before she directly responded to his very different "Letter to a Young Contributor" published there, in April, 1862.

When the Civil War started, Higginson volunteered although he was thirty-eight. After some restless waiting for instructions, he was appointed Colonel of the First South Carolina Volunteers in 1862. This was the first regiment recruited from former slaves to fight for the Union Army. Until then, even liberals in the north, as Higginson well knew, had been afraid to put guns in the hands of blacks. He later wrote, "We had touched the pivot of the war. . . . Till the blacks were armed, there was no guarantee of their freedom. It was their demeanor under arms that shamed the Nation into recognizing them as men." Higginson served with his regiment until he was wounded and forced to retire.

After the war he strongly supported the fight for equal pay for

Black soldiers, and was outspoken in his disgust at the injustices of
Reconstruction. But the years mellowed his radicalism, and although
his *Army Life in a Black Regiment*, written after the fact, in 1869, is
an important document in Civil War history, although there is no doubt
of Higginson's anti-slavery position, the book was unfortunately influenced by the period's anthropological view of different racial tempera-
ments. Here, black soldiers are docile, innocent, infinitely humble. It
is hard to believe that this same man only a few years earlier had written "The Insurrection of Nat Turner."

During his years with the South Carolina Volunteers, Higginson
was intrigued by black music. He carefully recorded many of the words
to the spirituals and other slave songs he heard the soldiers singing.
A long article he wrote on black American folk songs in the June 1867
edition of the *Atlantic Monthly* is still cited today by music scholars.
But for Higginson's efforts, many of the words to these songs might
have been lost.

The members of Higginson's regiment seem to have been fond
of him. Years after the fighting, he received a letter from a former South
Carolina volunteer:

> I meet manny of the old Soldiers I Spoke of you–all hailed your name
> with that emotion (that become you) of the Soul when hearing of one
> who when in darkness burst light upon their pathway.

In April 1862 Emily Dickinson, a soul in the darkness of utter
poetic anonymity wrote to Higginson. That his prompt response saved
her in some crucial sense, she often told him. In 1869, seven years later
she wrote:

> You noticed my dwelling alone–To an Emigrant, Country is idle
> except it be his own. You speak kindly of seeing me. Could it please
> your convenience to come so far as Amherst I should be very glad, but
> I do not cross my Father's ground to any House or town.
>
> Of our greatest acts we are ignorant–
>
> You were not aware that you saved my Life. To thank you in per-
> son has since been one of my few requests.
>
>   (L330)

And ten years after that:

> Must I lose the Friend that saved my Life, without inquiring why?
> Affection gropes through Drifts of Awe–for his Tropic Door–
> That every Bliss we know or guess–hourly befall him–is his scholar's
> prayer–

(L621)

During the 1860s to a Life standing in Corners, to intellectually ambitious women, to blacks struggling for liberation, this influential and busy public speaker and man of letters, offered time, encouragement, and generous interest. But the same lack of imaginative intensity that blinded him to the metaphysical desolation stalking the Browning of "Childe Roland," caused him actively to dislike all of Melville's writing, and led him to say in a review of Whitman's second edition of *Leaves of Grass*, "Its nauseating quality remains in full force," also made him deaf to the rebellion, the act of lonely daring, in the poetry of Emily Dickinson. In his early days, rebel he indeed was, but he was a man of action, not of hesitation and skepticism. As a man of action, his overriding and enthusiastic optimism, made him a kind and generous person. At the point in time when Dickinson first wrote to him, he was in his prime. A Unitarian minister who had once been fired by his congregation, a rebellious agitator for the causes of Women's Rights, and Abolition, an outspoken advocate of human freedom who practised what he preached. He answered Emily Dickinson's letter at once.

*　　*　　*

After reading in the *Springfield Republican* that T.W. Higginson had left to lead his regiment in South Carolina, Emily Dickinson wrote him:

February 1863

Dear Friend

I did not deem that Planetary forces annulled–but suffered an exchange of Territory, or World–

I should have liked to see you, before you became improbable. War

feels to me an oblique place–Should there be other Summers, would
you perhaps come?

I found you were gone, by accident, as I find Systems are, or Sea-
sons of the year, and obtain no cause–but suppose it a treason of Progress–that dissolves as it goes. Carlo–still remained–and I told him–

> Best Gains–must have the Losses' Test
> To constitute them–Gains–

My Shaggy Ally assented–

Perhaps Death–gave me awe for friends–striking sharp and early,
for I held them since–in a brittle love–of more alarm, than peace. I
trust you may pass the limit of War, and though not reared to prayer–
when service is had in Church, for Our Arms, I include yourself–I,
too, have an "Island"–whose "Rose and Magnolia" are in the Egg,
and it's "Black Berry" but a spicy prospective, yet as you say, "fascination" is absolute of Clime. I was thinking, today–as I noticed, that
the "Supernatural," was only the Natural, disclosed–

> Not "Revelation"–'tis-that waits,
> But our unfurnished eyes–

But I fear I detain you–

Should you, before this reaches you, experience immortality, who
will inform me of the Exchange? Could you, with honor, avoid Death,
I entreat you–Sir–It would bereave

> Your Gnome
>
> (L280)

When she fired off this eloquent and bitterly ironic letter–a terse
cry of paralysis from a northern woman's consciousness in wartime;
left with her dog, her parents, children, and other women; left with
information indirectly supplied by newspapers, and her own improbable
position in a hieratic patriarchal system; left with these things; and over-
weening ambition–she enclosed a poem.

> The Soul unto itself
> Is an imperial friend–
> Or the most agonizing Spy–
> An Enemy–could send–
>
> Secure against it's own–
> No treason it can fear–

Itself–it's Sovereign–of itself
The Soul should stand in Awe–

(683)

*　　　*　　　*

"My life had stood–a Loaded Gun–" peers voluptuously through its own chronology straight into our time. This austere poem is the aggressive exploration by a single Yankee woman, of the unsaid words–slavery, emancipation, and eroticism. In the fifth and toughest verse, HIS foe's unnamed power to harm is emphatically erased. None even *stir*–the second time. The stoic Scout-Gun's Yellow-Bullet-Eye, is righteous, isolate, cyclopean, feminine. Kill-deer and Hawk-eye. Mary Rowlandson guarding God. In War's necessity supplier and suppliant are one.

*　　　*　　　*

VI

Though I than He–may longer live
He longer must–than I–
For I have but the power to kill,
Without–the power to die–
power] art

From first word to the last MY Life my art my power DIEs into rhymed order. Rhyme and meaning are one, death completes my life and makes it mine. Master is still sleeping, Gun still soliloquizing. Self will fight transformation, hold fast alert, unresting. Like Victory, Justice, Words, my Mind must be ready to change sides.

Late May 1863

Life is death we're lengthy at, death the hinge to life.
(L281)

Gun in My Life
 My Life in Gun
  My in The Owner
   The Owner in My
    Catherine in Heathcliff
     Heathcliff in Catherine
     Edgar in Tom
      Tom in Edgar
       Panther in Boone
        Boone in Panther
        Doe in Rebecca
         Rebecca in Doe
          Killdeer in Deerslayer
           Hawk-eye in Kill-deer
            Serpent in Chingachgook
             Chingachgook in Serpent
              He in I
               I in He
                Childe Roland blowing Edgar's mad song.

           *   *   *

Inward and outward turning, the four lines of the sixth and last stanza of the poem are a mirror-maze in the process of Metamorphosis.

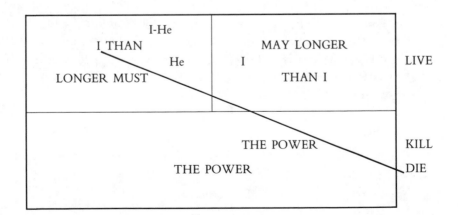

Inside the mirror–the second two lines–the poem makes its transump-
tive turn. Master-Owner is gone–mere Gun. In the third stanza, Gun
took God's place as guard. "Which, Sir, are you and which am I/Upon
an August day?" (124) Now Dickinson assumes in art her own power.
The soul is a bride. Joined together, she and her precursor-lover are
mighty as the greatest mystery which is Death.

> The Mountains–grow unnoticed–
> Their Purple figures rise
> Without attempt–Exhaustion–
> Assistance–or Applause–
>
> In Their Eternal Faces
> The Sun–with just delight
> Looks long–and last–and golden–
> for fellowship–at night–
> (757) 14 in fascicle 34
>
> 6. just] broad
> 8. fellowship] sympathy–

*   *   *

Candor–my Preceptor–is the only wile.
(L450)

Emily Dickinson often switched roles in her letters to Thomas
Wentworth Higginson. In the third letter she wrote him, she started
off with effusive thanks:

June 7th 1862

Dear Friend.

Your letter gave no Drunkeness, because I tasted Rum before–
Domingo comes but once–yet I have had few pleasures so deep as your
opinion, and if I tried to thank you, my tears would block my
tongue– . . .
Would you have time to be the "friend" you should think I need?
I have a little shape–it would not crowd your Desk–nor make much
Racket as the Mouse, that dents your Galleries–
If I might bring you what I do–not so frequent to trouble you–
and ask you if I told it clear–'twould be control, to me–

Then switched roles in midstream:

> The Sailor cannot see the North–but knows the Needle can–

She, tearful little mouse, who had just been begging for "control," was now the sailor (Columbus) and Higginson was simply the needle on her compass (Gun).

> The "hand you stretch me in the Dark," I put mine in, and turn away–I have no Saxon, now–

Still changing, the letter became a poem for eight lines, until shifting into prose again she took his hand and turned away asking:

> But, will you be my Preceptor, Mr Higginson?
>
> (L265)

When Higginson's first wife died many years later, he received this:

Sept 1877

Dear Friend.
    If I could help you?

> Perhaps she does not go so far
> As you who stay–suppose–
> Perhaps comes closer, for the lapse
> Of her corporeal clothes–

Did she know she was leaving you? The Wilderness is new– to you. Master, let me lead you.

(L517)

Only a year later, The *Springfield Republican* on 1 December 1878 announced Thomas Wentworth Higginson's engagement to Mary Potter Thatcher of Newton.

Dear Friend,

> I heard you had found the Lane to the Indies, Columbus was looking for–

There is no one so happy her Master is happy as his grateful Pupil.

The most noble congratulation it ever befell me to offer–is that you are yourself.

Till it has loved–no man or woman can become itself–Of our first Creation we are unconscious–

> We knew not that we were to live–
> Nor when–we are to die–
> Our ignorance–our Cuirass is–
> We wear Mortality
> As lightly as an Option Gown
> Till asked to take it off–
> By his intrusion, God is known–
> It is the same with Life–
>
> (L575)

The game of hide-and-seek, the charade of domination, obedience, disobedience, and submission–continued for as long as they corresponded. Her last letter to him, written very shortly before she died, was in response to a report in The *Springfield Republican* that he had been prevented by illness from attending a meeting of the Browning Society. Obliquely run, the circle ends where it began:

> *early May 1886*
>
> Deity–does He live now?
> My friend–does he breathe?
>
> (L1045)

Characteristically she closed their twenty-four year correspondence with a question.

*   *   *

As always with Emily Dickinson, there can be no final interpretation of the poem, especially to this most mutable and riddling verse. On some level, Gun needs to keep re-assuring herself and us, of "His," her nameless Master/Owner's superiority. During the nineteenth century, a wife was her husband's property, and a woman lacked the power to vote in a Democracy. Not to be able to vote leaves one powerless to effect change. To die is to change utterly. All her life Dickinson was acutely sensitive to the loss of freedom a married woman was expected to accept without question. So was Emily Brontë. Catherine Earnshaw Linton chose to die, but her ghost lived on, a wraith, scratching at the window wild nights on the heath, pleading to be let back in, to her loved lost original home.

*   *   *

In 1883, after her eight-year-old nephew Gilbert's sudden death from typhoid, Emily Dickinson wrote to her old friend Mrs. Holland:

Sweet Sister.

Was that what I used to call you?
I hardly recollect, all seems so different—
I hesitate which word to take, as I can take but few and each must be the chiefest, but recall that Earth's most graphic transaction is placed within a syllable, nay, even a gaze—
The Physician says I have "Nervous prostration."
Possibly I have—I do not know the Names of Sickness. The Crisis of the sorrow of so many years is all that tires me—As Emily Brontë to her Maker, I write to my Lost "Every Existence would exist in thee—". . .
"Open the Door, open the Door, they are waiting for me," was Gilbert's sweet command in delirium. *Who* were waiting for him, all we possess we would give to know—Anguish at last opened it, and he ran to the little Grave at his Grandparent's feet—All this and more, though *is* there more? More than Love and Death? Then tell me it's name!
(L873)

*   *   *

A Poet's words like the sun against glass, may recoil false meaning back on herself, artificial definition, that smears true light with antic reflection. The end of a poem, like the end of a life, releases language into the sovereignty of abdication.

Soft as the massacre of Suns
By Evening's Sabres slain

(1127)

1. massacre] [massacre]s
2. Sabres] Sabre

For the journey of a soul across the distance to being's first breath, true existence is in the Abyss. *Yes*, trusted to night and silence.

*   *   *

Lear. Come, good Athenian

Glou. No words, no words: hush

*   *   *

Let us now recall that most moving last scene, one of the culminating points reached in modern tragic drama: "Enter Lear with Cordelia dead in his arms." Cordelia is Death. Reverse the situation and it becomes intelligible and familiar to us – the Death-goddess bearing away the dead hero from the place of battle, like the Valkyr in German mythology. Eternal wisdom, in the garb of the primitive myth, bids the old man renounce love, choose death and make friends with the necessity of dying. . . . But it is in vain that the old man yearns after the love of woman as once he had it from his mother; the third of the Fates alone, the silent goddess of Death, will take him into her arms.

(Sigmund Freud, "The Theme of the Three Caskets" pp. 78–79)

Freud's silent Goddess of Death would have been a stranger to Emily Brontë and Emily Dickinson. In a universe identified with Absence, the forbidden territory between man, woman, and God, has torn love from the world. Love waits outside beyond remembrance or caring. If the Goddess of Death was unfamiliar, so was a masculine Father who required Obedience without question. Both women resisted such domineering demands for submission and they resisted comfort and confidence.

> The Zeros taught Us–Phosphorus–
> We learned to like the Fire
> By handling Glaciers–when a Boy–
> And Tinder–guessed–by power
>
> Of Opposite–to equal Ought–
> Eclipses–Suns–imply–
> Paralysis–our Primer dumb
> Unto Vitality–

(689)

7. dumb] numb–

*   *   *

The subject and conflict of *Wuthering Heights* and "My Life had stood–a Loaded Gun–" is complete union with another soul and absolute separation. Catherine and Heathcliff are each other's central source. They contain, define, and defy one another, and everyone else around them. In Dickinson's poem, this same unity is at the core of identity– Gun and hunter, My and Master. In verse five, Gun must go on loving and guarding. Who is knower, who known–sure opinion will surely break down. Sadism knocks down barriers between an isolate soul and others. Violence forces reaction. That unity of souls may be linked to sadism is the sad riddle of the world. In these works of imagination by two women, in Mary Rowlandson's Narrative, in Shakespeare's four History Chronicles of the Wars of the Roses, in *Lear*, *Macbeth*, *Othello*, *Timon*, in all of the Leather-Stocking tales, and in Browning's "Childe Roland" vulturism is the human condition. Voice throws heart against flint.

*   *   *

At the end of beginning, Gun affirms the aggression in God's yellow eye of Creation. Still she will not give into pessimism. Death is a generative force. If Redemption is separated from us eternally in time and space, this division must be eternally re-crossed. Lear, Gloucester, Heathcliff, Chingachgook, Natty Bumppo and Roland meet their own deaths joyfully. For the narrator of "My Life" the power to die *is* life.

> I peeped in. Mr. Heathcliff was there–laid on his back. His eyes met mine so keen, and fierce, I started; and then, he seemed to smile.
>
> I could not think him dead–but his face and throat were washed with rain; the bed-clothes dripped, and he was perfectly still. The lattice, flapping to and fro, had grazed one hand that rested on the sill–no blood trickled from the broken skin, and when I put my fingers to it, I could doubt no more–he was dead and stark!
>
> I hasped the window; I combed his black long hair from his forehead; I tried to close his eyes–to extinguish, if possible, that frightful, life-like gaze of exultation, before any one else beheld it. They would not shut–they seemed to sneer at my attempts, and his parted lips, and sharp, white, teeth sneered too!
>
> (*Wuthering Heights*, ch. 34)

Exultation is the going
Of an inland soul to sea–
Past the Houses,
Past the Headlands,
Into deep Eternity–

(76, v. 1)

*   *   *

Sola, sola, wo ha, ho, sola!
  (Epigraph from Shakespeare used by
  Cooper in *The Last of the Mohicans*)

PROMETHEUS, father of the Arts and Sciences stole fire from Zeus
as a gift for man and was tortured for it. He lighted his torch at the
wheel of the sun.

Said Death to Passion
"Give of thine an Acre unto me."
Said Passion, through contracting Breaths
"A Thousand Times Thee Nay."

Bore Death from Passion
All his East
He–sovreign as the Sun
Resituated in the West
And the Debate was done.

(1033)

*   *   *

1864]   I noticed that Robert Browning had made another poem, and was
          astonished–till I remembered that I, myself, in my smaller way,
          sang off charnel steps. Every day life feels mightier, and what we
          have the power to be, more stupendous.

(L298)

A woman who is no longer youthful but who remains a virile
poet hemmed in by centuries, as Stevens rightly said, that have a way
of being male, needs courage, discipline, humor, and freedom of spirit.
"Hamlet wavered for all of us" said Dickinson; and like Hamlet/
Shakespeare she looked right into the nature of things/words, straight

through,–to the fearful apprehension that there was no Truth, only
mystery beyond mystery. To subjugate her master, Death, by means
of Art, was a possible solution. One that required dedication and preci-
sion. For the strenuous mental activity she was engaged in, she needed
peace of the familiar and sheltered isolation. Luck provided her with
a devoted family that protected her privacy, a large house, a room of
her own, and money. Her niece, Martha Dickinson Bianchi:

> Once in that happy place I repeated to Aunt Emily what a neighbor
> had said–that time must pass very slowly for her, who never went
> anywhere–and she flashed back with Browning's line:
> Time, why, Time was all I wanted!

*   *   *

> There they stood, ranged along the hill-sides–met
> To view the last of me, a living frame
> For one more picture! in a sheet of flame
> I saw them and I knew them all. And yet
> Dauntless the slug-horn to my lips I set
> And blew. *"Childe Roland to the Dark Tower came."*
> (v. 34)

Poetry is the great stimulation of life. Poetry leads past possession
of self to transfiguration beyond gender. Poetry is redemption from
pessimism. Poetry is affirmation in negation, ammunition in the yellow
eye of a gun that an allegorical pilgrim will shoot straight into the quiet
of Night's frame. Childe Roland at the moment of sinking down with
the sun, like Phaeton in a ball of flame, sees his visionary precursor
peers ringed round him waiting

To Edward (Ned) Dickinson   *mid-may 1880*

Phoebus– "I'll take the Reins."

Phaeton.

(L642)

WORKS QUOTED

Adams, Henry. *The Letters of Henry Adams,* ed. J. C. Levenson, Ernest Samuels, Charles Vandersee, Viola Hopkins Winner. Cambridge: Harvard Univ. Press, 1982. 6 volumes.

Aquinas, Thomas. *An Aquarian Reader,* ed. Mary T. Clark, New York: Image Books/Doubleday & Co. 1972.

Bianchi, Martha Dickinson. *Emily Dickinson Face to Face: Unpublished Letters with Notes and Reminiscences by her Niece Martha Dickinson Bianchi.* New York: Archon Books, 1932; rpt. 1970.

The Bible. King James Version.

Brontë, Charlotte. *Memoir of Emily Jane Brontë.* Oxford: Basil Blackwell, 1934.

Brontë, Emily. *The Complete Poems of Emily Jane Brontë.* New York: Columbia Univ. Press, 1941.

Brontë, Emily Jane. *Five Essays Written in French,* tr. Lorine White Nagel. Texas: The Univ. of Texas Press, 1948.

Brontë, Emily. *Wuthering Heights,* ed. David Daiches. Harmondsworth, Middlesex: Penguin books Ltd., 1965.

Brontë, Emily and Anne. *The Poems of Emily Jane Brontë and Anne Brontë.* Oxford: Basil Blackwell, 1934.

Brown, John. *The Life and Letters of John Brown, Liberator of Kansas, and Martyr of Virginia,* ed. F. B. Sanborn. New York: Negro Universities Press, co. 1969.

Browning, Elizabeth Barrett. *The Complete Poetical Works of Elizabeth Barrett Browning.* Boston: Houghton Mifflin and Co., 1900.

Browning, Robert. *Men and Women.* Boston: Ticknor and Fields, 1856.

Browning, Robert. *Men and Women,* London: Chapman and Hall, 1855.

Calvin, John. *Institutes of the Christian Religion,* tr. John Allen. Philadelphia: Presbyterian Board of Christian Education, 1902.

Cixous, Helene. "The Laugh of the Medusa." In *New French Feminisms: An Anthology,* ed. Elaine Marks and Elizabeth de Courtivon. Amherst: Univ. of Massachusetts Press, 1980, 247–255.

Cooper, James Fenimore. *The Last of the Mohicans: A Narrative of 1757*. New York: Harper and Row, 1965.
The Deerslayer or, the First War Path, New York: Stringer and Townsend, 1854.

Crashaw, Richard. *Oxford Book of English Verse*, ed. Arthur Quiller-Couch Oxford: Clarendon Press, 1930.

Dickens, Charles. *David Copperfield*. London: Oxford University Press, 1948.

Dickinson, Emily. *Letters*, ed. Thomas H. Johnson. Cambridge: Harvard Univ. Press, 1958. 3 volumes.

————————. *The Manuscript Books of Emily Dickinson*, ed. R.W. Franklin Cambridge: Harvard Univ. Press, 1981. 2 volumes.

————————. *The Poems of Emily Dickinson*, ed. Thomas H. Johnson. Cambridge: Harvard Univ. Press, 1958. 3 volumes.

Donne, John. *Poetical Works*, ed. Herbert Grierson. London: Oxford University Press. 1968.

Edwards, Jonathan. *Representative Selections with Introduction, Bibliography and Note* by Clarence H. Faust and Thomas H. Johnson, New York: Hill and Wang, 1962.

Eliot, George. *Essays of George Eliot*, ed. Thomas Pinney. New York: Columbia Univ. Press, 1963.

Ellmann, Richard. *James Joyce*. New York, London, Toronto: Oxford Univ. Press. 1959.

Emerson, Ralph Waldo. *The Complete Works of Ralph Waldo Emerson*. Boston and New York: Houghton Mifflin Co., 1876.

Flint, Timothy. *The First White Man of the West, or The Life and Exploits of Col. Dan'l Boone*. Cincinnati: Anderson, Gates and Wright, 1858.

Freud, Sigmund. *Character and Culture*, ed. Philip Rieff. New York: Collier Books Inc., 1963.

Gilbert, Sandra M. and Susan Gubar. *The Madwoman in the Attic: The Woman Writer and the Nineteenth Century Literary Imagination*. New Haven: Yale Univ. Press, 1979.

Higginson, Thomas Wentworth. "Letter to a Young Contributor." In *Atlantic Essays*. Boston: James Osgood and Co., 1871.

Keats, John. *The Poetical Works of John Keats*, ed. Heathcote William Garrod. London: Oxford Univ. Press, 1939.

Keats, John. *Letters of John Keats*, ed. Robert Gittings. London: Oxford Univ. Press, 1970.

Leyda, Jay. *The Years and Hours of Emily Dickinson*. New Haven: Yale Univ. Press, 1960.

Mather, Cotton. *Magnalia Christi Americana*. Hartford: Silus Andrus and Son, 1853. 2 volumes.

Mather, Increase. *The History of King Phillip's War*, ed. Samuel G. Drake. Boston: New England Historic-Geneological Society, 1862.

Milton, John. *Oxford Book of English Verse*, ed. Arthur Quiller-Couch. Oxford: Clarendon Press, 1930.

New French Feminisms: An Anthology, ed. and with intro. by Elaine Marks and Isabelle de Courtivon. Amherst: Univ. of Massachusetts Press, 1980.

Nietzsche, Friedrich. *Ecco Homo: How one Becomes What one is*, tr. R. J. Hollingdale. Harmondsworth, Middlesex: Penguin Books Ltd., 1979.

Rowlandson, Mary. *The Narrative of the Captivity and Restoration of Mrs. Mary Rowlandson*, First printed in 1682 in Cambridge *Massachusetts*, & London, *England*. Now reprinted in *Fac-simile*. Whereunto are annexed a *Map* of her Removes, *Biographical* & *Historical Notes*, and the last *Sermon* of her husband Rev. Joseph Rowlandson. Lancaster, Mass: 1903.

Shakespeare, William. *The Comedies, Histories, Tragedies, and Poems of William Shakespeare*, ed. Charles Knight. London: Charles Knight and Co., 1843.

Spenser, Edmund. *The Faerie Queene*, ed. Thomas P. Roche, Jr. Harmondsworth, Middlesex: Penguin Books Ltd., 1979.

Stevens, Wallace. *The Necessary Angel, Essays on Reality and the Imagination*. New York: Knopf, Inc. and Random House, Inc. 1951.

Thoreau, Henry David. *"The Last Days of John Brown," The Writings of Henry David Thoreau*, vol IV. Boston: Houghton Mifflin Co., 1906.

Thoreau, Henry David. *A Week on the Concord and Merrimack Rivers*, with a foreword by Denham Sutcliffe. New York: New American Library, 1961.

Webster, Noah. *An American Dictionary of the English Language*, New York: Harper and Brothers, 1854.

Williams, Roger. *A Key to the Language of America*, Reprinted Providence, 1936

Williams, William Carlos. *In the American Grain*. New York: New Directions Publishing Corp., 1956.

Zukofsky, Louis. *Bottom: On Shakespeare*. Austin, Texas: The Ark Press, 1963.